A Guide to Becoming A Vocational Expert with the Social Security Administration
2nd Edition

By Asheley D. Wells, MS, CRC &
Gerald K. Wells, Ph.D., CRC

A Guide to Becoming A Vocational Expert with the Social Security Administration 2nd Edition

© 2020 Copyright - Commonwealth Education Publications

ISBN-13: 9798615743559

By Asheley D. Wells, MS, CRC &
Gerald K. Wells, Ph.D., CRC

Cover Design and Book Layout – Shri Henkel

Table of Contents

Introduction

For over 50 years the Social Security Administration has used rehabilitation consultants from outside of the Agency to help their administrative law judges make decisions of entitlement in their Social Security Disability Insurance (SSDI) and Social Security Income programs. Many of these professionals are rehabilitation counselors; some are psychologists; and some are educators coming from a variety of related occupations. But all of these rehabilitation consultants serving as government contractors with the Social Security Administration have a specialized knowledge of disability and the impact of a physical or mental condition upon a person's ability to work. The Agency has labeled these professionals <u>*Vocational*</u> <u>*Experts*</u>*.*

The vocational expert is not an employee of the Social Security Administration. Vocational experts are government contractors, independent of the disability process, and their testimony is expected to be impartial. Nor does the vocational expert have responsibility for deciding the outcome of the claimant's case; all determinations of the court are made by an administrative law judge (ALJ). During a disability hearing VE's, as they are called, respond to hypothetical questions about vocational issues posed by the ALJ to help the judge make a decision about a claimant's ability to work. Finally, while the VE is asked about jobs in the national economy, employment or job placement is not the goal. The consideration of a disability hearing is cash payments made to persons unable to work.

On the other hand, the vocational expert plays an important part in the disability determination process. Based upon the medical and other records, as well as the testimony of claimants, and possibility the testimony of medical experts and others, administrative law judges make a vocational assessment from the evidence provided to them. Usually, the vocational expert is asked by the ALJ to classify the claimant's past work in terms of the skills and level of exertion. And, in response to hypothetical questions from the judge, the VE provides opinion evidence testimony, in a hypothetical form of questioning, about a claimant's ability or inability to work under different situations. The vocational witness is considered by the court to be an expert based upon his/her knowledge of disability and work.

Consulting as a vocational expert is an expanding area of opportunity for professionals with a background that involves an understanding of a disabling condition and the impact of a disability upon a person's ability to work. You do not have to know it all when you start; all practicing VE's have learned much of their knowledge of disability, and the process for determining disability, on the job. What is necessary is that you accept the challenge and be willing to become dedicated to continuous learning. While consulting in this area is not full-time work (rehabilitation consultants are expected to have an outside business or occupation), consulting as a VE provides challenging work, scheduled on days the expert chooses to serve as an expert in the court, in an occupation that makes a difference in the lives of persons with disabilities.

The Guide to Becoming a Vocational Expert with the Social Security Administration is written from the viewpoint of the vocational expert. The authors are practicing VE's under contract with the Social Security Administration to provide consulting services. The content of this book is meant to provide an understanding of what it is like to be a vocational expert in Social Security hearings.

The second edition of the Guide to Becoming a Vocational Expert with the Social Security Administration lists and explains some of the changes taking place in the Social Security Administration over the past three years, since the publication of the first edition, that affect the disability adjudication process, and, in particular, changes that affect the vocational expert. But the main difference between the 2015 edition and this second edition is the expanded number of examples of functional limitations ALJ's may direct to a VE's in hypothetical form of questioning. These examples, mostly taken from actual hearings, provide an analysis of the source, or how these limitations might develop from the evidence, and give

suggestions of occupations and jobs that a vocational expert may use to address specific limitations in function.

In this book you will be carried through the 5-step process the administrative law judge uses to determine disability; you will meet the persons who normally participate in disability hearings, including the administrative law judge, the hearing reporter, the medical expert(s), the claimant representative, and, most important, the claimant; you will follow the hearing process used to evaluate a claimant's disability; you will see how the VE evaluates a claimant's past work, with examples taken from real situations; you will see ways VE's use the Dictionary of Occupational Titles and other research to evaluate the past work of claimants; you will examine the criteria that makes up the hypothetical questions asked by the administrative law judge; you will see how vocational experts respond to questions from attorneys during cross-examination; you will be presented with selective hypothetical questions and the kinds of responses typically given by vocational experts; and you will see, by example, some of the jobs and occupations VE's cite to address specific client limitations.

What it is Like to be a Vocational Expert with the Social Security Administration

In the literature of disability law, a vocational expert, as opposed to say an expert witness, is more narrowly defined as "a person giving testimony in a disability hearing". Providing testimony on disability is a familiar role for most rehabilitation counselors. In fact, one primary role they have in serving persons with disabilities relates to their skill in determining the impact of a disabling condition upon a person's ability to work. But the professional practice of rehabilitation counseling involves a wider range of duties and responsibilities, such as counseling, case management, and job placement. Rehabilitation counselors can be vocational experts. Many of them serve in that role as part of their professional practice. But the designation of <u>vocational expert</u> is specific to the function served by a consultant with the Office of Hearing Operations (OHO) of the Social Security Administration.

In the past VE's were used more sparingly than today; in fact, in some federal jurisdictions, they were not used at all. But in the litigious environment we live in today, most ALJ's rely upon the advice and testimony of vocational experts to help them decide the majority of adult cases. Why is this? By profession an ALJ is an attorney. While most of the judges have a keen knowledge about vocational matters, they are not prepared by education or training to address vocational issues in a court of law. They need the presence of an expert on vocational issues to classify work in terms of skill and exertion, to address vocational areas that need explanation, and to help the judge understand the impact of a claimant's disability upon their ability to work, both their past work and other work that may be available to a claimant.

Do you picture yourself as a vocational expert in a court room with a daunting judge in a black robe, looking like Darth Vader, peering down upon you from a raised platform, while across the table sits a smug attorney waiting for you to make one slight mistake before eating your liver? So many rehabilitation counselors refuse to take advantage of becoming a vocational expert because they conjure up an image similar to this when considering becoming a VE. But it is not like this at all - - for a variety of reasons:

(1) The courtroom is not like you see on television. Admitting evidence into the file for consideration and taking testimony under oath are about the only really formal procedures. Federal Rules of Civil Procedure and Federal Rules of Evidence are not stringently applied. In fact, the ALJ makes a deliberate attempt to place everyone who will testify at ease at the beginning of the hearing. As one administrative law judge explains in his opening

remarks: "our proceedings here today are more like a conversation around the dinner table".

(2) The work is challenging and the growth you experience in learning to become a VE easily carries over to other work with injured and disabled people, even in job placement, making you a much better professional. Possibly the most professional activity a rehabilitation counselor does is to determine the impact of the limitations caused by a disabling condition upon a person's ability to work. All other services provided by rehabilitation counselors in relation to work depend upon the accuracy of this determination.

(3) This work, places rehabilitation counselors on the cutting edge of professional practice. Not only is serving as a VE lucrative (most VE's exceed the national average salary for rehabilitation counselors) but there is no better preparation for expert consultation in other court settings than the experience VE's gain in a Social Security hearing.

(4) If you have a degree or degrees in rehabilitation counseling or a related field, your skills are uniquely shaped to this kind of work. Rehabilitation

counseling is the only counselling profession where disability and work form a primary body of knowledge within the profession. Of course, if you plan to apply to become a VE and continue a sustained relationship with the Social Security Administration, you will need to acquire work experience that involves counseling of persons with disabilities in work situations and job placement.

(5) Unlike the negative images you may entertain, most of the judges and the attorneys respect vocational experts and the testimony they provide during the hearing. The testimony of the vocational expert, as we shall see, is crucial to the determination the administrative law judge has to make in determining a claimant's disability or ability to work.

(6) And don't rule out the personal prestige that goes along with being an expert! This challenging work does wonders for your self-esteem.

Electronic Records for Experts (ERE)

By definition "an expert is a person who is permitted to testify at a trial because of special knowledge or proficiency in a particular field that is relevant to the case". By this definition, a vocational expert is "a person" who has a "special knowledge or proficiency" in the "vocational field" of knowledge and testifies at a "legal hearing" on "vocational and work-related issues".   Each vocational expert is chosen by the Social Security Administration and labeled "expert" because of their special knowledge of disability and work and their ability to offer opinion evidence on the impact of a disabling condition upon a person's ability to work. Upon acceptance by the Social Security Administration, the professional comes under contract with SSA and is considered a vocational expert.

To become a government contractor as a vocational expert with SSA, you need to apply at the closest Office of Hearing Operations. Once you have received notice from OHO that you are on their roster of experts, the Office will call you by phone or contact you by email to determine your availability for a particular time period. Usually the case technicians at OHO ask what days you are available for a particular month. You then, in turn, let them know which days that month you can serve. In a return call or email sent to you, a case technician at OHO will assign hearing days during a month to you. On a given day you will be asked to testify usually on from four to seven cases.

Your next step is to receive notices in the mail for each case that lists the name of the claimant, the date, time, and location of the hearing, the time period your testimony will cover, and the name of the ALJ hearing the case. The notice will also say:

"Your presence throughout the hearing is desired since your testimony will be based, in part, on the testimony given by the claimant and any other witness, including a medical advisor, if needed. Copies of the pertinent exhibits tentatively selected for inclusion in the record of this case are available to you either

- by compact disc (CD) that will be mailed under separate cover if not enclosed with this notice or

- Electronically at

  http://secure.ssa.gov/ERECA/MEVE:01View .

The directions then go on to describe how you can access the ERE system now used by SSA. As the notice indicates, the Social Security Administration is moving away from providing its experts with a CD containing evidence in the case to giving VE's electronic access to the disability case data base of the Social Security Administration. Many of the experts under contract with SSA have already moved to using the ERE system.

Over the past 30 years the Office of Hearing Operations of the Social Security Administration has updated their procedures for sending information about claimants for review prior to the hearing. Some years ago an entire file would be sent to experts by mail. Once an expert had reviewed the case he/she would return the case file to the post office and mail the file back to OHO. (Needless to say the risk of losing a file was always a concern) Some years later OHO stopped sending the entire file by mail and began to send copies of only the vocational information from the file. For the past 20 years or so the files have been placed on a compact disc and sent to an expert by mail along with notices for the date of the hearing and an agenda.

Beginning in 2017 SSA began moving to a new system called the Electronic Records for Experts (ERE). Under ERE experts go directly into the Social Security Administration's data base, identify the files they need to review, and download those sections to their personal computer.

Usually when an expert requests sections from the file under ERE, the information is available within an hour or less. The expert then can either print the sections, download the sections into a thumb drive for use on their laptop or personal computer, or place the information in a folder on a laptop and carry the computer to disability court on the date of the hearing.

The Social Security Administration has printed easy-to-use instructions on how to access and use the electronic files. These instructions are available at the local OHO office once an expert, under contract, has passed the required security measures, and has been placed on the roster of experts for a local OHO office. Case technicians are available, upon request, to help with questions expert may have about ERE or how to use ERE to retrieve case information. The ERE system represents advanced technology, and places SSA on the cutting edge of innovation in media presentation technology.

Reviewing the Record

Vocational Experts with the Social Security Administration are paid for the time they spend studying the case and participating in the hearing. An expert is not paid for his/her testimony. One of the first things that an expert must understand is that experts are independent witnesses, present during a hearing or by phone, to offer opinion evidence on vocational and work-related matters. Experts must confine their opinions to their expertise in their own professional field. However, the Social Security Administration has established a framework for vocational issues and the expert must cast their testimony within that framework. This is difficult for some experts. Board-certified medical experts with years of experience in the medical field sometime become a train wreck in the courtroom, offering opinions well outside of their expertise and experience. As a result, they compromise their testimony and undermine the opinion evidence they are giving in the case.

When an expert first views the records in a claimant's file, the sheer volume can be overwhelming. You have before you a record of all the medical evidence and decisions made in the case to that point, all the correspondence the Social Security Administration has exchanged with the claimant and the claimants' representative, the vocational and work records, and medical records and reports. As vocational experts must limit their opinions to their own area of expertise, the only records they need to review are those related to vocational and work-related issues.

From the perspective of the VE, the most important vocational records in the case file needing review are forms and reports prepared under the guidance of SSA staff in the local Social Security offices. These records are found in Section E of the case file under the title of *Disability Report – Adult,* and the *Work History Report.* (The entire Section E is available to vocational experts through ERE). Each of these reports has a space to list the jobs a claimant has performed over the past 15 years. The *Work History Report* has, as well, a space to describe the job duties and the exertion levels of each job the claimant has performed. In order to offer opinion evidence on vocational matters during a hearing, the vocational expert is expected to have reviewed these files and other relevant vocational information contained in the case file before coming to the hearing.

The information the vocational expert takes from the case file review forms a vocational profile, a snapshot of the claimant's vocational factors of age, education, and work experience. Age, education, and work experience are the three (3) key factors that go into making up a person's vocational profile. Vocational experts use a combination of these same three factors in making an assessment of a claimant's ability to work and a determination of the kinds of jobs that person can do. (In the Appendix we have provided a summary of these vocational factors. The reader may wish to review the information in the appendix before moving forward).

A Case Review Worksheet

When reviewing the vocational information in the file, VE's must decide what information they need to take from the records to place before them during the hearing.

We have prepared a sample **Case Review Worksheet** to help the vocational expert in reviewing the past work before coming to the hearing. There is no standard form for this review. Each VE will have their own method for recording information from the vocational records. However, most of the case review worksheets contain the same essential information. The beginning expert can feel free to set up their own sample work sheet based upon the sample given here.

Once complete, the Case Review Worksheet can be placed in a folder along with the hearing notice for the day of the hearing. A vocational expert will normally have 4 to 7 hearings on a given day; therefore, it is imperative to keep all the information separate for each claimant. Most VE's refer to information on the worksheet throughout the hearing. To demonstrate, we will fill in the work sheet below with information taken from the fictitious case of Cornelius Jones. Here is the vocational profile we prepared for Cornelius Jones:

Cornelius Jones is 47 years old, having been born June 2, 1972. He attended high school through the 11th grade at Mt View High School in Morehead City, North Carolina. While he was in high school, he was in the vocational program and attended classes to become a carpenter. Cornelius has had no other formal education or vocational training. He left high school in 1989 to go to work as a flagger for the North Carolina State Highway Commission. Two years later he went to work at Jones Construction with his father, a construction contractor. He worked for a year at Jones Construction as a general laborer and then as a rough carpenter. He was working as a carpenter with Jones Construction when his accident occurred. He has had no other jobs during the past 15 years.

On July 1, 2014 while working at a construction site, Cornelius fell from scaffolding to the ground 15 feet below. As a result of the fall, he broke his left arm, shattered his right knee, and experienced a herniated disc in his lower back at the L4-L5 lumbar sites. In spite of extensive conservative medical treatment, and an operation on his back, he has continued to have back pain which he rates at a level 9 on a 10-point pain scale. He now feels that he is unable to continue his work as a carpenter or perform any other gainful activity. Cornelius has applied for Social Security Disability Insurance (SSDI) and Social Security Income (SSI). He is represented by Howard Shank of the law firm of Shank and Finster.

Case Review Worksheet

Name: Cornelius Jones   **Age: 47 Years**

DOB: 6/2/72

Date of Onset: 7/1/14   **Education: 11**
years (no special education)

Complaints: Herniated Disc, Back Pain, Knee Pain

Military Service: No

Vocational Training: Carpentry in high school

Representative: Howard Shank

Past Work:

Job Title: Flagger

Exertion Level: Light/SVP-2

Employer: State of NC

Dates: 1990-1991

DOT Designation: 372.667-022

Job Title: General Laborer

Exertion Level: Very Heavy/SVP-2

Employer: Jones Construction

Dates: 1991-1992

DOT Designation: 869.687-026

Job Title: Carpenter

Exertion Level: Medium/SVP-7

Employer: Jones Construction

Dates: 1992-2016

DOT Designation: 860.381-022

Possible Work Alternations:

Job Title:	Exertion levels	DOT Designations

Notes:

Case Review Worksheet

Name: CORNELIUS Jones   Age: 42   DOB: 6/2/72

Date of Onset: _____

Complaints: DISC
                   BACK PAIN
                   KNEE PAIN

Education: 11 Years

Military: No

Vocational: CARPENTRY

Attorney: Howard Shank

Past Work:

Job Title	Employer	Dates	Exertion	DOT #
Flagger	State of N.C.	90/91	L-2	372.667-022
Laborer	Jones Const	91/92	VH-2	869.687-026
Carpenter		92/16	M-7	860.381-022

Alternative Work:

Job Title	Exertion	DOT	Job Numbers

Notes/Hypothetical Questions:

You will notice that the Case Review Worksheet (above) provides space to list the Dictionary of Occupational Titles (DOT) designation for each of the jobs performed in the past. Administrative Law Judges often request a DOT code to make sure that the VE and the ALJ are talking about the same job. The ALJ at Step 4 is seeking information to determine if the claimant can perform any of the jobs done in the past.

The form also provides space to list job alternatives. While reviewing the records from the case before and during the hearing, the VE may consider alternative employment, jobs a claimant may be able to perform given the vocational profile. If so, there is space to list some of the possibilities. Finally, the VE may wish in the "Notes" section to list the limitations the ALJ and other experts provide that form the substance of hypothetical questions if the case goes to Step 5 of the sequential evaluation.

Background: The Emergence of the Vocational Expert in Social Security Hearings

When Congress passed the original Social Security Act of 1935 creating retirement benefits for persons over 65 years of age, there was already discussion about expanding the program to provide wage-related cash benefits to workers who became permanently and totally disabled before the age of 65, now 67. At that time the proponents of a disability program argued that "the permanently disabled were the only major class of people needing protection that did not receive it under the Social Security Act and yet no other group was more completely dependent or in a more desperate economic situation". (7, pg.1)

But it would be another 20 years before a national disability program would become a reality. One of the main reasons for the delay was concern over the difficulty of making disability determinations; that is, the subjectivity of determining whether a person was truly disabled. Concerns about the subjectivity in disability determinations have continued to follow the program to this very day.

On August 1, 1956 President Dwight D. Eisenhower signed into law the Amendments to the Social Security Act establishing the Social

Security Disability Insurance (SSDI) program. The Social Security Income (SSI) program was established by Congress in the 1967 Amendments and implemented in 1974, eighteen years after the creation of the SSDI program. Social Security Disability Insurance (SSDI) is an insurance program. Employees contribute portion of their earnings each payday to purchase insurance in the event they become unable to work.   The money goes into a trust fund that insures cash payments in the event they become unable to work. The contribution is part of a FICA tax; current amount of FICA tax taken from an employee's paycheck is 7.65%.   Employers match their worker's contribution. Persons who are self-employed contribute (by a formula) both the employer's share and the employee's share of the tax. Social Security Income (SSI), on the other hand, is a need-based program providing for cash payments to persons unable to work and have not contributed substantially to the SSDI program.

In the year before the passage of the 1956 Amendments, the Commissioner of Social Security had appointed a Medical Advisory Committee (MAC) to formulate a policy for evaluating disability. The panel set forth medical criteria for evaluating specific impairments with the level of severity for each. The panel also suggested that factors such as age, education, training and experience were important in the evaluation of disability even though the new law did not specifically require consideration of these factors. One recorded statement from the Medical Advisory Committee said "in determining whether an individual's impairments make him unable to engage in such activity (work), primary consideration is given to the severity of his impairment. Consideration is also given to such other factors as the individual's education, training, and work experience". (7, pg.3)

Following passage of the 1956 Amendments to the Social Security Act, the new law experienced problems in the courts. Numerous court cases challenged the practice of making determination of disability based upon medical evidence alone. In a sense the way the guidelines were set up, adjudicators simply looked at the medical evidence and if in their own judgment the disability was total, then that was that. The converse was also true. If a person's impairments did not meet the requirements of the medical evidence in the adjudicator's mind, the applicant was turned down for benefits.

As a consequence of court challenges, congressional committees during the Lyndon B. Johnson administration took notice of the trends in case law and in the Social Security Amendments of 1967 made it clear that a claimant may be found disabled "only if his physical or mental impairment or impairments are of such severity that he is not only unable to do his previous work but cannot, considering his age, education, and work experience, engage in any other kind of substantial gainful work that exists in the national economy regardless of whether such work is in the immediate area in which he lives, or whether a specific job vacancy for him, or whether he would be hired if he applies for work".(7,pg.5)

The courts had made it clear that in order to deny a claim for disability, the adjudicator for the Social Security Administration had the burden of proof to address the vocational issues in each case and show there were jobs a claimant could perform in spite of their physical or mental limitations.   Initially, the Social Security Administration attempted to address the vocational issues in disability cases by relying upon "selected government and industrial studies", but the courts rejected this approach because the reports were "speculative and theoretical in determining whether there were employment opportunities available to disability claimants". As a result of these court challenges, the SSA determined that a more specific and reliable way to address whether or not a person can work was to employ independent vocational experts who could provide live testimony related to a claimant's "particular and highly individual situation". (8, pg.2)

The Social Security Administration has continued to use vocational experts in cases appealed to the Office of Hearing Operations (OHO) for roughly the past 50 years. During that time, the Social Security Administration has withstood numerous legal challenges to the use of vocational experts; in contested cases, the courts have been relatively uniform in recognizing vocational expert testimony as an acceptable way to address work-related issues in disability cases. Today, administrative law judges with the Office of Disability Adjudication and Review (ODAR) rely upon the testimony of vocational experts in most adult cases during disability hearings on appeal.

The 5-Step Process for Disability Determination

Both for the Social Security Disability Insurance program (SSDI) and for the Social Security Income program (SSI) a person is awarded cash benefits if their disability is of such severity to prevent them from working. The process for evaluating disability is identical for both programs.

Congress has defined disability as "the inability to engage in substantial gainful activity by reason of any medically determinable physical and mental impairment which can be expected to result in death or which has lasted or can be expected to last for a continuous period of not less than twelve months". (1, pg.2) To make disability determinations based upon this definition, the Social Security Administration has adopted a five-step sequential process that considers the uniqueness of a claimant's impairment or impairments.

It is important to understand how the word sequential is used in the process of defining disability. The term sequential means a claimant cannot proceed from one step to the next until it is determined that he/she is disabled at the previous step. For example, the administrative law judge will proceed to Step 5 to consider alternative work only after making a determination at Step 4 that the claimant cannot do his/her past work. The burden of proof rests upon the claimant to show that at each step from one through four during the sequential process, he/she meets all requirements for disability. At step five the burden of proof shifts to the Commissioner of Social Security and requires that the adjudicator (ALJ) provide evidence that the applicant can or cannot work.

Step 1: The first step of the five-step sequential evaluation process is for the adjudicator to determine whether the individual is currently engaged in substantial gainful employment. The term substantial gainful employment is defined in monetary terms. For instance, from 1980-1989 a claimant's gross income became substantial gainful employment when that person earned $3600 a year; in 2018 that amount is $14,160 or $1100 a month. If a claimant has earned more than the established amount during a given year, that person is not eligible for benefits.

Step 2: At the second step the adjudicator has to determine whether or not the individual has an impairment or combination of impairments that are severe. In its regulations the Social Security Administration has defined severe as "a medically determinable impairment or combination of impairments that significantly limits a person's physical or mental ability to do basic work-related activity". (15, pg.14) For an impairment to be <u>medically determinable</u> the condition must have been determined by clinical or laboratory diagnostic studies or by other acceptable medical means. According to federal regulations governing the program, "the standard for assessing severity at Step 2 is medically only. Vocational factors, such as age, education and work experience are considered by the judge at this step but they are more important at Steps 4 and 5 of the sequential evaluation process". (15, pg.13) The impairment must have lasted, or be expected to last, for 12 months.

Step 3: If a claimant seeking disability has an impairment that meets the durational requirements of 12 months and meets, and equals, one or more of the list of medical impairments provided by the Social Security Administration, the claimant is found disabled at Step 3 without considering the claimant's age, education, and work experience. The Listing of Impairments contains 14 separate body systems and the conditions the claimant must meet to be declared disabled under each listing. These listings include:

- 1.00 Musculoskeletal Systems;

- 2.00 Special Senses and Speech;

- 3.00 Respiratory System;

- 4.00 Cardiovascular System;

- 5.00 Digestive System;

- 6.00 Genitourinary Impairments;

- 7.00 Hematological Disorders;

- 8.00 Skin Disorders;

- 9.00 Endocrine System;

- 10.00 Impairments affect multiple body systems;

- 11.00 Neurological;

- 12.00 Mental Disorders;

- 13.00 Malignant Neoplastic Diseases; and

- 14.00 Immune System.

The List of Impairments used by the Social Security Administration is contained in the book titled *Code of Federal Regulations* (CFR). The Code of Federal Regulations is provided by OHO to administrative law judges, medical advisors serving as medical experts in Social Security hearings, and claimant representatives.

If, on the other hand, a person has a severe, medically determinable impairment which though not meeting or equalling the criteria in the listing of impairments, prevents the person from doing their past relevant work, the Administrative Law Judge must determine whether or not the person can do other work. At Steps 4 and 5 of the sequential process, the determination is made based upon a claimant's ability to perform his/her past work and other work that exists in significant numbers in the national economy.

Step 4: Making the disability determination at Step 4 involves consideration of the person's residual functional capacity (RFC) and the vocational factors of age education and work experience. A claimant's RFC is formed by an initial assessment of a person's physical and mental abilities and limitations and the kinds of work that person can do within those limitations (see Appendix "Vocational Factors").

At Step 4 the Administrative Law Judge looks at the claimant's ability to perform his/her past work. If it is determined that the claimant is able to perform past relevant work (work within the past 15 years), then the process stops right there and benefits are denied. In analyzing the past work of claimants at Step 4, the administrative law judge relies on the testimony of the vocational expert to only a limited extent. In most instances the ALJ has the vocational expert classify the past work of claimants in terms of the skill required to perform the job and the level of exertion. The

Dictionary of Occupational Titles is the source for determining the skill and the level of exertion of each job. From the classification provided by the vocational expert, the ALJ determines whether or not the claimant can perform any of the jobs done over the past 15 years. If the ALJ cannot make a determination from the classification, the judge will give a hypothetical question and then ask the VE if the person could return to the past work the VE has described given the limitations outlined in the RFC.

Step 5: Under the sequential evaluation, if a claimant cannot perform his/her past relevant work, the evaluation process continues to Step 5. At Step 5, the regulations that govern the program say SSA must determine the existence of a significant number of jobs in the national economy which the claimant is able to perform: "for the purposes of determining a claimant's ability to engage in work other than past relevant work, work is considered to exist in the national economy when there exists a significant number of jobs in one or more occupations, that have requirements the claimant is able to meet with his/her physical or mental abilities and vocational qualifications". (15, pg.18)

At Step 5 the ALJ relies heavily upon testimony from the vocational expert. It is the VE who provides jobs for an ALJ to consider at Step 5. Using a hypothetical format, the ALJ requests from the vocational expert a representative number of jobs that exist in the national economy, the expert believes, the claimant in the hearing can perform within a given RFC.

The opinions expressed by vocational experts are formed from a review of the records provided to them, by listening to the testimony of claimants and others during the hearing, by using vocational information derived from a variety of sources, especially the *Dictionary of Occupational Titles*, (12) and from personal experience gained while working with injured and disabled clients in employment situations. The testimony of the VE is "crucial to the proceedings because neither the administrative law judge nor the claimant possess the ability to analyse the exertion and skill required in particular employment situations". According to one critic, "the testimony of the vocational expert is the foundational block of the SSA disability determination process, because, without it, a complete, accurate, and reasonable decision would not be possible". (9, pg 367)

Persons Appearing in a Social Security Hearing

If claimants live within 75 miles of the hearing site, disability hearings are held at the Office of Hearing Operations (OHO). Satellite hearing sites are also provided in order to hold hearings for claimants who live in more remote locations. In the recent past, hearings were held in other temporary sites, including Social Security field offices, other federal buildings, and even motel and hotels. In the past, Administrative Law Judges would regularly have to travel to these alternate sites for hearings carrying recording equipment and boxes of cases. Vocational experts and hearings reporters would also travel to these sites. Not much anymore.

Today, hearing sites have become more uniform and most hearing rooms are designed exclusively for Social Security hearings. Even alternate sites are more uniform; motels and hotel rooms are used sparingly. More uniformity has become necessary, in part, because of the expanding use of teleconferencing. Normally, when hearings are held using teleconferencing, vocational experts and the ALJ are in the main OHO location while claimants and their representatives, along with the hearing reporter, are at the remote site. Innovation in teleconferencing within SSA has removed much of the travel for both experts and the ALJ. (The Illustration below provides an idea of a typical arrangement in most hearing sites).

Hearing Room

The typical courtrooms have a formal arrangement of the furniture, forming a "T", a setting very similar to the more formal rooms in the district court setting (without the jury box). The judge's desk and chair stand behind a wooden rail on a raised platform. The hearing reporter normally sits to one side of the judge. A long table forms the base of the "T". The claimant sits at the end of the "T" facing the judge. Usually, a large television screen is attached on the wall behind the claimant for use in teleconference hearings. The claimant's representative, if there is one, sits to the left of the claimant at the table and the vocational expert is seated on the right. Witnesses on behalf of the claimant are often sworn in and then sequestered while the claimant testifies. Occasionally, persons (friends, relatives) who are not testifying are allowed to remain in the hearing room for moral support for the claimant.

An Administrative Law Judge presides over the hearing. The ALJ has a broader range of duties than a trial judge. The ALJ has the challenge of protecting both the government's interest and the interest of the claimant while, at the same time, rendering an impartial decision. The cases come to the ALJ on appeal from the processing bureau, the Disability Determination Services (DDS). The hearings are *de novo* - meaning the ALJ is not bound by previous determinations. The ALJ makes a completely new and independent decision based upon the medical and other evidence in the case, the testimony obtained at the hearing, and application of the evidence to the Social Security Law.

A hearing reporter is also present. The hearing reporter is responsible for setting up and operating the recording equipment, taking notes, and making sure that the hearing runs smoothly. In the past the hearing reporters would gather new evidence a claimant or the claimant's representative may have brought with them on the hearing day and deliver the new information to the judge for review. Seldom now do attorneys or claimants bring new evidence to court on the day of the hearing. SSA has now adopted "a five-day rule" and all evidence must be presented to the court five days in advance. Both the claimant and the claimant's representative are required to have all evidence submitted 5 days before the hearing for the ALJ to have time to examine the evidence prior to the hearing

On the day of the hearing the hearing reporter has to obtain from a representative, if there is one, a fee agreement and a right to representative form before the hearing can begin. If the claimant is unrepresented, the hearing reporter may provide the claimant his/her file to review.

The hearing reporter usually ushers the claimant and others into the hearing room. At the beginning of the hearing, at the judge's direction, the reporter turns on the recording equipment and announces the opening of the hearing by saying "on the record". At the close of the hearing, at the judge's direction, the reporter announces that the hearing is "off the record" and turns off the recorder. At the request of the ALJ, the reporter may stop the recording at any time during the hearing. The normal hearing length is 45 minutes to an hour.

Not all claimants are represented by council. Most are, but a claimant has the right to choose whether to have a representative. Claimant representatives are mostly attorneys, but some are non-attorneys. The non-attorneys are usually persons familiar with disability law and the disability determination process. If claimants are not represented by someone of their choice, at the beginning of the hearing the ALJ will advise them of their rights to representation and describe what a representative can do for them. The statement below is typical.

Rights to Representation

"Let me take a moment to cover your rights to representation. Since you are not represented by counsel today, I want you to understand that you have the right to be represented during this hearing by an attorney or non-attorney. This person will help you obtain information about your claim, submit evidence, explain medical terms, make requests, protect your rights, present the evidence in a light favorable to your case, and make any requests or give any notice about the proceedings here before me. A representative may not charge or receive a fee unless we approve it. A representative is not normally paid unless you are awarded benefits and then they may only accept 25% of your back benefits or $10,000, whichever is less. However, a representative may charge you for certain expenses, such as obtaining and copying medical records. Some legal service organizations offer free legal representation if you quality under their rules. This is usually need based. Of course, you may also proceed today without a representative. If you do so, I will obtain the relevant medical and non-medical records and evidence in your case, and I will question you during the hearing about your claim. Do you fully understand your rights to representation"?

Should the claimant decide to obtain the services of a representative, the ALJ will normally grant to them a one-time postponement to a later date for them to get a representative.

The main point of the hearing is for claimants to prove to the Administrative Law Judge that because of a disabling condition, they can no longer work. To help the ALJ make a favourable decision, claimants or their representatives submit medical evidence from a variety of treating sources. When vocational issues contribute to the disabling condition, claimants or their representatives may submit other evidence like school records or employer statements. Claimants may also choose to have family members, friends, medical professionals, counsellors and others appear at the hearings to testify about their disabling condition.

Medical experts may also appear at the hearing or by phone. Medical experts are either expert in the field of medicine or expert in the field of mental health. Experts from the field of medicine are physicians, usually retired physicians, but still with current medical credentials, such as a board certification in their medical specialty (internal medicine, orthopaedics, etc). The testimony of the physician concerns the physical aspects of a claimant's disability. Appearing at the hearing or by phone may be a psychiatrist or psychologist to testify on the mental and emotional aspects of a claimant's disability. Usually, experts in mental health are practicing professionals.

Medical experts examine evidence in the records and offer an opinion as to whether a claimant meets or equals the Listings of Impairments, a Step 3 determination. Therefore, the testimony of the medical expert will precede that of the vocational expert. Like a vocational expert, medical experts are paid by the government but are expected to offer impartial testimony. Should the testimony of the medical expert determine that the claimant meets or equals the medical conditions listed in the List of Impairments, the testimony of the vocational expert may not be needed.

Finally, appearing last in the hearing are vocational experts. The vocational expert may appear either in person or by phone. As noted earlier, the vocational expert testifies on the vocational issues in a case, including classification of a claimant's past work in terms of skills and exertion required of that work, transferability of work skills for claimants over 50 years of age, and possible jobs a person with the same background and work experience of the claimant can perform given a series of hypothetical situations formulated by the ALJ.

Timothy Field and Jack M. Sink in *The Vocational Expert* (1981) describe the qualifications needed by vocational experts. They say to qualify as a vocational expert with the Social Security Administration "a vocational expert is expected to possess current and extensive experience in counselling and/or job placement of adult, handicapped people with a work history. The experience should include (1) utilization of standardized occupational material, such as the *Dictionary of Occupational Titles*; (2) an understanding of the structure and function of work, and the concept of transferability of skills; and (3) the ability to evaluate age, education, and prior work experience in light of residual functional capacities, as specifically related to industrial and occupational trends and local labour market conditions is necessary". (6, pg.5) As noted, the testimony of the vocational expert is impartial and based upon the expert's own education, professional experience, and understanding of the Social Security Law.

The Hearing Process

A typical hearing begins with the ALJ and the attorney discussing any housekeeping issues, such as new, last-minute evidence the attorney would like entered into the file, or a request to the ALJ by the claimant's representative to keep the file open after the hearing to submit new evidence. Once on the record with the recorder operating, the Administrative Law Judge usually begins with an introduction or opening statement explaining the nature of the hearing process and what is expected of the claimant.

An ALJ uses the information from "The Judges Procedure Manual" to formulate an opening statement. There is variation in the content of the opening statement as most administrative law judges personalize their opening address to the court. The following is an actual opening used by an administrative law judge. The opening was chosen for inclusion in this text because the content contains most of the essentials needed in an opening statement. As observed, this particular opening statement has had the effect of making claimants feel more comfortable and at ease at the beginning of the hearing. The names of the persons in this excerpt are fictitious.

Administration Law Judge's Opening Statement

"We are ready to proceed in the case of Roger Simpkins. I am Judge William Atkins. I have been assigned to hear your case. As you are probably aware, there have been prior decisions in your case. I am not bound by those prior decisions. Rather, I get the chance to take a whole, fresh look at your case. My decision will be based upon the evidence in the file, and testimony that comes before us today. And if the record is held open for additional evidence, the decision would be based upon those records as well. After that, I will make a decision. It will be in writing, and it will be mailed to you and to your representative.

I'd like to emphasize that this is your hearing. If you have any questions you wish to ask or recognize something that is not being brought to my attention, I ask that you not be bashful. Let me know before the end of the hearing because we want to make sure this is a full, fair hearing. As you may gather from the microphones before you, we are making an audio recording of the hearing. The microphones are sensitive. We do ask that you speak up so whatever you say is picked up and made a part of the record. I trust you will do that, because if we don't get a good recording, they may make us come back and do this all over again, which we would all like to avoid. Operating the equipment is our contract hearing reporter, Susan Francis. She takes notes and tries to keep me on track.

As you may observe from the surroundings, this is not a formal hearing. The rules of evidence don't apply. We don't get to do these cases like you see on television – no Perry Mason, no Law and Order, no Boston Legal. Rather, we like to believe this is more like a conversation around the dinner table. Even though this is an informal proceeding, however, there are a few formalities. I am required to enter into evidence the exhibits in the file. I am also required to take evidence under oath. I will be swearing you in shortly. After we get done with these preliminary matters, I will let the representative make any opening statement he deems appropriate. After that, I will question you; your representative will question you. After that we will discuss your medical situation with Dr. Haney. Then we will turn to the vocational expert and discuss with her your past work and work background and I will also pose some questions to him about a hypothetical individual. That will bring our hearing to a close.

We are here to determine whether you are disabled within the guidelines of the Social Security Act. Disability under the Act is defined as the inability to engage in any substantial gainful employment based on a physical or mental impairment that results in death or which has lasted or is expected to last 12 months. I will cover all material facts to determine if you are eligible for benefits under the Social Security Law. Material facts include any work you have done since your onset date, the severity of your impairments, and the effect of any impairment upon your ability to do your past work or any other work that exists in the national economy based upon your age, education, and work experience. That is a long-winded way of saying we are here to determine if you are disabled, but that is it in a nutshell. Do you have any questions how we will proceed today?"

The introduction raises two technical points that may not be clear to most of us. The judge says that he is not bound by prior decisions. When a case comes before an Administrative Law Judge at the OHO appeal level, the case has been reviewed twice by consulting physicians and others working for the Disability Determination Service (DDS) and a determination was made in those reviews that the claimant was not disabled. The hearing is at the minimum a third review. The ALJ is stating up front that he does not have to base his decision upon the results of those former decisions; his decision will be a wholly new decision. This is the only time in the disability process that a claimant will meet a live person making the decision. At all other levels of appeal within the Social Security Administration, the determinations are made by file review. If the claimant receives an unfavorable decision from the ALJ, there is another level of appeal within the Social Security Administration. That level of appeal is the Appeals Council. But that level of appeal is also a file review.

Also, in the introduction the ALJ says that the judge will make the decision based upon the testimony and the evidence in the file. In hearings before an administrative law judge, the greatest weight toward making the disability decision goes to the opinions and medical evidence of the claimant's treating physician(s). Other evidence, such as the opinions of the vocational expert, receives a lesser weight in these decisions.

Following the opening statement, the ALJ admits exhibits into the file, and asks the representative if any of the claimant's impairments meets or equals a listing in the List of Impairments. In other words, may the case be determined at Step 3. The Judge may also ask the representative for a summary or theory of the case, i.e. reasons why the evidence shows their client meets the requirements of the Social Security Law and is eligible for benefits under the Law.

Afterward, the ALJ introduces the persons participating in the case and defines their role in the hearing. The introductions usually go something like this: "I am William Atkins; I am the judge who has been assigned to hear and decide your case. Seated to my left is the hearing reporter, Susan Francis. She takes notes and keeps the hearings running smoothly. On my right is a vocational expert, Ms.

Childress. She isn't employed by the Social Security Administration and has no interest in the outcome of the case. She will be classifying your past work and answering questions about other work that may exist within the national economy". If there are other experts at the hearing, the Judge Houser would introduce them as well: "We also have Dr. Haney, a medical doctor, and Dr. Mullinax, a psychiatrist with us today. Both have reviewed your medical records and may be asked to provide testimony based on their professional experience in reference to your case. These medical experts are not employees of the Social Security Administration and they have no interest in the outcome of our proceedings today".

After introducing the participants at the hearing, the ALJ administers the oath to those who will be testifying at the hearing. Before administering the oath, the ALJ first addresses the claimant, saying "Do you have any objection to taking an oath? (Presumably the claimant's answer is no). "Then if you and our expert(s) Ms. Childress (VE), Dr. Applebee (ME), and Dr. Mullinax (ME) would please stand and raise your right hands. "Do you swear to tell the truth, the whole truth, and nothing but the truth under penalty of perjury?" (Everyone says "I do").

The ALJ may elect to begin the questioning of the claimant or decide to allow the claimant's representative to begin asking the questions. In either scenario, the examination usually begins by asking the claimant some personal matters, such as height, weight, marital status, type of dwelling (house, apartment, mobile home), who lives in their household, and whether she/he has performed any work since the onset of disability. The questions that follow begin with the medical issues in the case. Among the issues raised will likely concern, if appropriate, a claimant's past history of drug or alcohol use, or periods of incarcerations. Under Social Security Law, the ALJ cannot award benefits to a person while that person is incarcerated; nor will the ALJ award benefits to a person if drugs or alcohol are the primary cause behind the disabling limitations that prevent the claimant from working.

At the conclusion of the questions from the judge and the claimant's presentation of the case, the administrative law judge usually turns first to the medical expert(s), if medical testimony is needed in the case. Whether or not to use a medical expert is a decision made by the judge hearing the case. If medical experts are to appear at the hearing or by phone, the first matter under consideration is for the judge to ask the claimant, and/or the claimant's representative, if they are willing to accept the opinions of the medical witness as that given by a medical expert. Unless the claimant or the claimant's attorney has reservations about the credentials of the medical expert, the ALJ declares the medical witness an expert in the case. This is a very important point. The judge will not accept the testimony of an expert witness unless the witness testifying is recognized by the court as an expert in his/her professional field.

Most often, the first question addressed to the medical expert is whether or not the claimant's medical impairments meet or equal the conditions provided in the "List of Impairments". In other words, the ALJ is asking the medical expert if a favorable decision can be made at Step 3 of the sequential analysis. If the claimant's medical condition does not meet or equal the requirements of the listings in the Listings of Impairments, the ALJ may then ask for the medical expert's analysis of the case records. If the medical expert states that the claimant's conditions are not severe enough to preclude work, the judge may ask experts to construct their own residual functional capacity (RFC) based on their examination of the evidence. Vocational experts need to take note of the medical expert's RFC because some of the judge's questions to the vocational expert later in the hearing will likely be based upon those physical or mental restrictions the medical experts at the hearing present in their RFC.

The analysis then moves into Step 4 and Step 5. In the order of progression the testimony of the vocational expert logically follows the presentation by the medical experts. The VE may be present to provide testimony or provide testimony by phone.

The judge begins the questioning of the vocational expert by asking the VE if the resume on file with the Social Security Administration is current and up to date. The ALJ will then ask the VE if there is any reason, he/she cannot testify as an impartial witness. Following these procedural questions, the ALJ turns to the claimant's representative and asks if there is any objection to having the VE present in the hearing or by phone to testify as an expert on vocational matters. With the up-to-date resume in the file and the acceptance of the claimant and/or the claimant's attorney, for the purposes of this case, the judge then declares the vocational witness an expert witness on vocational matters.

Having the claimant's representative accept the VE as a vocational expert in the case and having the judge declare the vocational witness an expert on vocational matters is an important milestone in the case. From this point forward, as far as this case is concerned, the VE no longer has to worry about questions which draw attention to his/her professional background, or questions about their qualifications to serve as an expert witness on vocational matters. The VE is an expert and any questioning from this point forward will be about the case and the VE's opinions in the case.

Qualifying the Vocational Expert in a Disability Hearing

To summarize, before hearing the testimony of the vocational expert, the ALJ will ask the VE if the resume on file and in the record is correct and up to date. After an affirmative response from the VE, the judge will turn to the claimant or the claimant's representative and ask if the representative is willing to stipulate that the VE is an expert on vocational matters during the hearing. The response from the claimant's representative and the claimant is almost always affirmative. The ALJ then says something to this effect: "I accept the VE in this case as an expert on vocational issues".

For the vocational expert this is an important moment in the hearing. In addressing the question "do you accept the VE as an expert on vocational matters?" to the claimant or the claimant's representative, the judge is giving the claimant or the claimant's representative the opportunity to ask questions regarding the credentials of the vocational expert. Once the claimant and the representative accept the VE as an expert in the hearing, administrative law judges do not usually allow questions about the background of the VE, inquiries about such things as the expert's academic education, professional experience, invited presentations, publications, memberships in national or local associations, or the status of the expert in their professional field. For the purpose of the hearing, the VE is an expert in the vocational field. Subsequent questions will only concern the testimony of the VE regarding their classification of the past work, their responses to hypothetical questions about alternative work, and their clarification of the testimony they have provided during cross examination.

As noted earlier, disability hearings under Social Security do not adhere strictly to the rules of evidence. Once a professional is chosen to serve as an expert, only the ALJ can decide otherwise. (This almost never happens). But most of us are familiar with what experts go through to establish their credentials during personal injury cases in other courts where the rules of evidence are more strictly applied. After having been grilled about professional credentials by opposing attorneys in civil cases, providing vocational testimony in a Social Security courtroom often seems like a moment of relief. So, it is natural for an inexperienced vocational expert, particularly in the early going, to feel a little uneasy during the time that the ALJ is presenting the expert's credentials to the court.

But, on a personal level, VEs need to remind themselves that once the judge during a disability hearing accepts the VE as an expert, their credentials are no longer an issue. VEs can and should turn their attention away from themselves to the real purpose of the hearing and the role they are to assume in the hearing.

Building a Vocational Profile

To begin their questioning, some administrative law judges ask the VE to provide a **vocational profile** of the claimant. The vocational profile overviews the claimant's age, education, and work experience. Let's take vocational profile information from the example under "A Case Review Worksheet"" on pages 22-24 to provide a typical response to the request by the ALJ for a vocational profile of a claimant:

VE: "Cornelius Jones is 42 years old; for Social Security purposes Mr. Jones is considered a younger person. He has an 11th grade education. This educational level for Social Security purposes is considered limited. He has worked for the past 15 years as a flagger, a general laborer, and a construction carpenter. The *Dictionary of Occupational Titles* lists a Flagger as light in exertion and unskilled with an SVP of 2 The DOT reference for this job is 372.667-022; a General Construction Laborer is very heavy in exertion and unskilled with an SVP of 2; the DOT reference for this job is 869.687-026; finally, the position of a Carpenter is medium in exertion and skilled with an SVP of 7; the DOT reference for this job is 860.381-022."

This information would normally come from your Case Review Worksheet if you used the worksheet during the hearing.

Classifying the Past Work

Before questioning the vocational expert at Steps 4 and 5, the judge goes through a list of prepared questions to establish the impartiality of the VE. The judge asks the VE: (1) have you and I had any discussion prior to the hearing concerning the merits of this case? (2) Do you know the claimant, or have you had any personal or professional contact with the claimant, the claimant's representative, or myself about the merits of this case prior to the hearing? (3) Is there any reason you cannot testify as an impartial expert on vocational matters in this hearing?" Given a negative response to each of these questions, the ALJ will likely conclude this line of questioning with an admonishment to the VE that if any of the responses to questions about the past work or hypothetical questions about other work conflict with the information provided in the *Dictionary of Occupational Titles,* the expert is to alert the court to the differences so that the conflict can be resolved.

Once the Administrative Law Judge has established the impartiality of the vocational expert, the questioning turns to the classification of the past work. Normally, the first question the ALJ asks of the vocational expert is to classify each job the claimant has performed over the past 15 years in terms of the skills needed to perform the jobs and the exertion levels of the jobs. Jobs outside of the 15 years are not considered relevant by the Social Security Administration. Classification of the past work provides an Administrative Law Judge with the vocational information needed to decide whether or not the claimant can perform his/her past work. This is Step 4 of the sequential analysis. If the judge decides the claimant can perform any of the jobs done in the past 15 years at Step 4, the analysis can stop there and the request for benefits will most likely be denied.

When requesting the vocational expert to classify the past relevant work, the judge expects the vocational expert to describe the past work in the way the work is listed normally in the *Dictionary of Occupational Titles* and how that work was actually performed as indicated in the records of the case and the claimant's testimony.

From the information provided by SSA and the testimony at the hearing, the vocational expert makes an assessment of the past work as that work was performed and reported by the claimant and compares that assessment with the descriptions of the jobs as they are listed in the *Dictionary of Occupational Titles*. Few vocational experts have heard the testimony of their colleagues or had any formal training, so the format VE's use in giving their vocational testimony may vary among different experts.

But while the style of presentation may vary among different experts, the information provided is much the same. We have chosen the work history from a different claimant. Matthew Higgins, to illustrate how a vocational expert may classify the past work of a claimant.

Let's suppose the claimant, Matthew Higgins, performed the job of a fast food worker from 1999 to 2003 at an Arby's restaurant in Baton Rouge, Louisiana. During the testimony Mr. Higgins says while on the job he served customers, made money transactions with the customers, cooked burgers and fries, and cleaned the tables during slow times in the restaurant. Most of this work had lifting requirements of less than 20 pounds. But at the end of the day, Mr. Higgins had to take trash to the trash bin. The trash barrels weighed about 45 pounds. The *Work History Report* listed 45 pounds as a weight he reported lifting on an occasional basis. The vocational expert may classify this job in the following way:

VE "Mr. Higgins worked as a Fast Food Worker in an Arby's Restaurant between 1999 and 2003. The reference to this work in the *Dictionary of Occupational Titles* is 311.472-010. As normally performed in the national economy, this work is light in exertion and unskilled. However, as listed in the *Work History Report* and testified at the hearing, Mr. Higgins had occasional lifting of 45 pounds. This would place the work as performed in the medium range. The skill level for the job, as performed, is unskilled work with a Significant Vocational Preparation (SVP) of 2 taking less than 30 days to learn the job duties and perform the work adequately".

Let's take another example. From 2004 to 2005 Mr. Higgins worked as a Dietary Aide in St. Marks Nursing Home in Baton Rouge. In this job he mostly carried trays of food to elderly patrons during meal time. But in the off hours he cleaned and mopped the floors and collected trash that required him to lift about 35 pounds. Once in a while, he testified, he had to empty bed pans and escort patients to the bathroom. He estimated that the patient care required him to lift over 75 pounds. This work may be classified in the following way:

VE: "Between 2004 and 2005 Mr. Higgins worked as a Dietary Aide in a nursing home where he had to carry trays to patrons in their rooms and sometimes had to help lift and carry these patrons. This work as listed in the *Dictionary of Occupational Titles* is medium in exertion with frequent lifting of 25 pounds and occasional lifting of 50 pounds. The DOT reference to this job is 319.677-014. But, as testified, he had lifting requirements occasionally of 75 pounds, placing the lifting level for this job, as performed, in the heavy range. Lifting in the heavy range has frequent lifting of 50 pounds and occasional lifting of 100 pounds. This is also unskilled work with a Significant Vocational Preparation (SVP) of 2 taking less than 30 days to learn the job duties and perform the work adequately".

Finally, there are some jobs that require workers to perform job duties that would satisfy the requirements for two or more separate occupations. These are considered <u>composite jobs</u> and in order to properly classify the work at Step 4, the VE will need to identify the two separate occupations that make up a composite job.

Composite jobs occur when a worker is employed by a single employer and the job tasks are not overlapping. The two jobs would be performed separately and on different shifts. Extra responsibilities an employee may be given from time to time or occasional add-on duties do not constitute a composite job. For instance, a front desk clerk may be asked to vacuum the lobby or clean rooms when the regular housekeepers are absent. These are just extra duties specific to that business location and would not be considered part of a composite job.

Convenience store cashiers, as opposed to larger chain stores, are often tasked with stocking the store with small items such as snacks and sometimes drinks which usually requires lifting no more than 20 pounds. Soft drink venders and sales representatives will stock the heavy cases of beer and soda. Because the convenience store cashier's responsibility includes light stocking, their job would not be considered a composite job of cashier and stocker. However, if a cashier worked in a large chain retail establishment and was given entire 4 to 8-hour shifts stocking one day and then another shift at the register on another day, the two jobs would combine to form a composite job.

In a recent hearing for Charlottesville, Virginia a claimant testified that she was both a head cook and a waitress for a restaurant in Bedford, Virginia. While she was on her shift in the kitchen, she cooked the meals, made up the daily menu, and assigned tasks to other kitchen workers. She did not have the authority to hire and fire other kitchen workers. On other days and shifts, she waited tables and cleaned the dining room. Her employer thought this arrangement was good because it gave the owner greater flexibility in assigning job tasks. This was clearly a composite job of a head cook and a waitress or server.

To classify a composite job, the VE needs to notify the judge the job is seen as a composite job with an assigned job title and reference number from the DOT for each occupation. <u>The VE will use the highest skill and the highest level of exertion from the components to classify the composite job.</u> In the previous paragraph, a housekeeper is normally unskilled and light in exertion. Conversely, a front desk clerk is normally semi-skilled and light. The composite classification for this job would be light and semi-skilled. A head cook in a restaurant is skilled work and medium in exertion, while a waitress or server is light and semi-skilled. The classification for this composite job is medium and skilled.

Sources of Information for Vocational Experts

The most obvious question that arises from the foregoing section about the classification of the past work is: where does the information come from to classify a person's past work and to address the hypothetical questions the ALJ will present to the VE. We will look at this information as it relates to the (a) **the classification of jobs**, and (b) the **characteristics the jobs**,

New vocational experts may feel overwhelmed by the vocational information needed to become a vocational expert, not to mention the ability to convert this information to vocational testimony. But the information is available to new vocational experts and others with a commitment to learning. All of us have become vocational experts by our education and knowledge of vocational and work related issues, work gained from practice in the field of rehabilitation. Along with our professional knowledge and experience, we have learned additional skills from our experiences in the courtroom.

Finally, in recent years our knowledge of jobs and work-related issues has been enhanced by developments in computer technology available to vocational experts that makes the information we provide through testimony now even more accurate and precise.

The process for analyzing the jobs and providing national statistics is not an exact science. As stated in *The Rehabilitation Counselor in Professional Practice*, the service we provide to the courts is more of an art than a science. Thanks to developments in this technology, you do not have to be an economist to analyze jobs and you can feel confident you are providing accurate information about jobs to the court.

Provided below are some of the basic sources of information vocational experts use to formulate their information for classifying jobs and providing responses to hypothetical questions during testimony in disability hearings.

(a) Classification of Jobs

The main source of information for the classification of jobs comes from the Department of Labor's *Dictionary of Occupational Titles*, the DOT. The 1991 edition includes a description and analysis of 12,741 occupations or categories of jobs in the United States. Below each of the jobs described in the DOT are some of the symbols needed to classify jobs, including the strengths (sedentary, light, medium, heavy, and very heavy), and the Specific Vocational Preparation (SVP), a number to represent the time it takes to learn a job and perform the job tasks adequately. These are the two most important components to the codes used to classify work during a disability hearing.

For example, let's suppose the claimant has listed the occupation of a Baker as a job he/she had performed in the past. The description of the occupation of a Baker can be found on page 368 of the DOT under the reference code of 526.381-010. Beneath the job description, the DOT lists the Strength as "H" with an SVP of 7, meaning that the job is heavy in exertion requiring 50 pounds of lifting frequently and 100 pounds of lifting occasionally. To learn the job duties and perform the work adequately at an SVP 7 takes one to two years. For most jobs the Strengths and SVP are all of the components of a job analysis needed to analyze and classify the past work during a disability hearing.

There is one little wrinkle in describing jobs in the courtroom today. You will remember that the ALJ usually concludes the opening statement to the VE with an admonishment something like this: "if any of your responses to questions about the past work or hypothetical questions about other work differ from the information provided in the *Dictionary of Occupational Titles,* please alert me to this problem so that the we can reconcile these differences." For most occupations there are no significant differences. The testimony is simply to provide the Strength and the SVP classification as given in the DOT for each job.

Problems arise occasionally, however, because the DOT was last published in 1991 and many of the jobs were last analyzed by a person viewing the performance of the job as far back as the late 1970's. *The Dictionary of Occupational Titles* (DOT) was first published by the Department of Labor in 1938 and updated periodically after that date until 1991. Although the DOT was not designed specifically for use by the Social Security Administration, SSA adapted its disability program to the DOT, incorporating many concepts and definitions from the DOT into its regulations and policies.

The Department of Labor stopped updating the DOT in 1991 and replaced the *Dictionary of Occupational Titles* with the *Occupational Information Network* (O'NET), a website designed for training and career exploration. The O'NET did not include the quantifiable factors for analyzing jobs, nor did it reflect the existence or incidence of work in the national economy. As a result, SSA did not consider a presentation of job information in the O'NET format to be defensible in a court of law. To many, presentation of the job information in the O'NET format would have been "theoretical and speculative" which the courts had rejected earlier when the SSI and SSDI disability programs were their formative stage. (See "Background: The Emergence of the Vocational Expert in Social Security Hearings" presented earlier).

In 2012 the Social Security Administration signed an interagency contract with the Bureau of Labor Statistics and two other agencies. SSA along with the participating agencies are currently in the process of coming up with a new format to be titled the Occupational Information System (OIS). Until this research and publication is complete, if vocational experts recognize differences between the DOT and the way they have observed a job performed, based upon their professional knowledge or experience, our suggestion is that they openly state these differences to the ALJ and proceed with their testimony.

(b) Characteristics of Jobs

Once again, the information for analyzing jobs comes from a Department of Labor publication. In 1991 the Department of Labor published *The Revised Handbook for Analyzing Jobs* which described the methodology job analysts with the United States Employment Service (USES) use to analyze jobs. *The Revised Handbook for Analyzing Jobs* defines and breaks down many of the terms used in job analysis.

The job descriptions for most of the jobs the USES analyzed were later published in the DOT. Beneath the description of the job in the

DOT were included some of the worker characteristics to assist vocational experts and others in analyzing jobs. In the section above we discussed two of these characteristics: Physical Demands and the SVP. In addition, the symbols under each job description in the DOT include information most helpful to career counselors, such as a reference to the *Guide to Occupational Exploration* which allows job counselors to cross-reference occupations with similar characteristics, interests and required job skills. The line beneath the job description in the DOT also notes the date the job was updated (DLU). The date last updated for the Baker position, discussed above, was 1980.

But there are physical demands and environmental conditions analyzed by the United States Employment Service not included in the *Dictionary of Occupational Titles* which vocational experts need to analyze jobs for the Office of Hearing Operations, (OHO). These worker trait characteristics include the **physical demand**: pushing and pulling (the only strength demand not included in the DOT); the **postural demands**: climbing, balancing, stooping, kneeling, crouching, crawling; **manipulative requirements**: handling, fingering, and feeling; and the many **environmental conditions** under which the work is performed. These come from another Department of Labor publication titled *Selected Characteristics of Occupations, 1992*. This publication contains worker trait characteristics for each of the 12, 741 DOT occupations.

In *Selected Characteristics of Occupations, 1992* Department of Labor analysts have rated the worker traits for each of the 12,741 jobs listed in the DOT by the frequency to which they appear during the normal workday. Each job listed in *Selected Characteristics of Occupations* is given one of four codes representing the frequency these factors normally appear during the workday:

Code	Frequency	Definitions
N	Not Present	Activity or condition does not exist
O	Occasionally	Activity or Condition exists up to 1/3 of the time
F	Frequently	Activity or Condition exists 1/3 to 2/3 of the time
C	Constantly	Activity or Condition exists 2/3 or more of the time

As an example, earlier we considered the position of a Baker. In the *Dictionary of Occupational Titles* (526.381-010) we found the position of a Baker was heavy in exertion and skilled with an SVP at level 7, taking one to two years to learn the job and perform the work adequately. In addition, *Selected Characteristics of Occupations, 1992* shows this position requires the physical demands of <u>frequent</u> reaching, handling, fingering and feeling, and

<u>occasional</u> stooping. Climbing, balancing, kneeling, crouching and crawling are <u>not present</u>.

For help in their testimony vocational experts are moving into the 21st Century with computerized programs to help locate and analyze data more accurately and efficiently. Perhaps the most popular, publically-available programs are Job Browser Pro by SkillTRAN, LLC, OccuBrowse by Vertek, and Osays, with SkillTRAN seemingly being the program of choice for vocational experts. The statistics compiled and presented by SkillTRAN, Occubrowse, and Osays have been recognized and accepted by the Social Security Administration. These computerized programs contain all of the data we have discussed in an easy to use format with job summaries and the worker trait characteristics for all 12,741 DOT occupations.

Questions to the VE in a Hypothetical Format

As described in the last section, classification of a claimant's past work occurs at Step 4 of the fact-finding process. Under the sequential evaluation process, as discussed earlier, if the ALJ determines a claimant cannot perform his/her past relevant work, the evaluation process moves on to Step 5. At step 5 the burden of proof shifts from the claimant to the Social Security Administration.

At Step 5 of the sequential evaluation, the ALJ must determine whether claimants, given their vocational profile and work background can make a vocational adjustment to other jobs that exist in significant numbers in the national economy. In order to deny benefits to claimants at Step 5, the ALJ for the Social Security Administration must identify a significant number of jobs in the national economy and determine the claimant is able to perform the jobs identified.

Regulations governing the administration of the Program state: "for the purposes of determining a claimant's ability to engage in work other than past relevant work, work is considered to exist in the national economy when there exists a significant number of jobs in one or more occupations, that have requirements the claimant is able to meet with his/her physical or mental abilities and vocational qualifications".

To make this determination, the administrative law judge relies heavily upon the testimony from the vocational expert. In the hearing the ALJ turns to the vocational expert and asks directly "can you identify specific occupations, and the numbers of jobs in the United States within those occupations, that the claimant can perform within their limitations given their age, education, and work experience".

To obtain this information in testimony from the VE, the judge moves from direct questioning to a hypothetical form of questioning. The hypothetical questions the judge asks the VE are just circumstances which mirror the information in the file, the claimant's testimony, the testimony of the medical experts, the job classifications of the VE, and the arguments the claimant's attorney constructs in the examination of the claimant. The hypothetical form of questioning is designed to leave the burden of interpreting the medical evidence to the Administrative Law Judge.

The questions in hypothetical form are the most confusing part of the hearing for most observers. Hypothetical questions about the vocational issues in the case are formulated by the Administrative

Law Judge and presented to the VE in several different scenarios. Usually, each succeeding scenario becomes more restrictive. Hypothetical questions create objectivity by allowing the judge to discuss a claimant's condition without specifically identifying the person sitting at the end of the table. Using a hypothetical format gives the judge choices for ultimately making the decision on disability. The hypothetical questions presented in this text are not comprehensive but are designed to provide a general understanding of the pattern delineated in the judge's inquiry.

Hypothetical questions are typically arranged and presented in this order:

1. **Vocational Profile**: age, education, and past relevant work.

2. **Physical Restrictions**: walking, standing, sitting, lifting, and pushing and pulling;

3. **Postural Limitations**: climbing, balancing, stooping, kneeling, crouching, crawling;

4. **Manipulative Limitations**; handling, feeling, fingering and reaching;

5. **Environmental Limitations:** exposure to weather, cold, heat, humidity, noise intensity levels, vibrations, atmospheric

conditions, moving mechanical parts, electrical shock hazard, radiation, explosion, hazard, toxic/caustic chemical hazard, or other environmental conditions.

6. **Psychological Limitations**; and

7. **Visual Limitations** (if any).

Sample Hypothetical Questions

Presented below are two examples of typical hypothetical questions posed by ALJ's to vocational experts. The first provides a sequence of hypothetical questions and VE responses designed to illustrate the process. The illustration uses a vocational profile of a 53-year-old construction laborer with a high school education, and complaints of severe chronic back pain. The hypothetical questions posed to the VE are:

ALJ: "Please assume a person with the same work background as the claimant and that I find from the evidence this hypothetical person can stand and/or walk for approximately 6 hours in an 8-hour day, and lift no more than 20 pounds at a time with frequent lifting or carrying of objects weighing up to 10 pounds. Would he be able to engage in his past work or, if not, could he engage in any other work?"

VE: "Under these limitations, the worker would not be able to perform his past work which was very heavy in exertion. This person would be reduced to a range of light work".

ALJ: "Please assume further, that I find from the evidence that the hypothetical person can sit for up to 6 hours in an 8-hour day, stand

and walk for no more than 2 hours in an 8-hour day, and lift up to 10 pounds. Can he engage in his past work? If not, can he transfer any skills to perform other skilled or semi-skilled work"?

VE: "The person would not be able to perform his past work. This person would be limited to sedentary work. Construction work is normally very heavy in exertion. The records and the testimony show that this person's past relevant work was performed at a heavy level of exertion. This work is unskilled and there can be no transferable skills from unskilled work".

ALJ: "Now, please assume that I find the claimants testimony about his back impairment to be credible, and that he can only sit for up to 3 hours, stand and/or walk for no more than three hours before experiencing severe pain, and lift no more than 10 pounds, and that he must lie down for at least 2 hours in any 8-hour period to relieve pain. If I accept this description of his limitations, could this person engage in his past relevant work"?

VE: "This person is reduced to a less than a sedentary level of work. Under these limitations this person would not be able to perform any full-time gainful employment. The need to lie down 2 hours in an 8-hour time period, furthermore, is not an accommodation that employers are generally willing to make".

Let's look at a more complex example of a hypothetical question, one that has multiple limitations. The hypothetical addressed to the For this hypothetical we are going to use a different vocational profile. This claimant is 46 years old with a high school education, and 19 years working experience as a waitress and a counter person in a laundry. The hypothetical addressed to the VE goes like this:

ALJ: "Please assume a hypothetical individual of the same age, education and past work the claimant has described and you have summarized. This person would be able to sit for six hours and stand and walk for six hours. Lifting is limited to 20 pounds occasionally and ten pounds frequently. She could occasionally climb, balance, stoop, kneel, crouch, and crawl. She would be limited to frequent fingering and handling. Avoid concentrated exposure to extreme heat, humidity and respiratory irritants. No exposure to hazards and unprotected heights. Because of frequent anxiety and panic attacks, this person would need to have only occasional interaction with the public. Poor concentration and memory loss, means this person needs routine, repetitive, unskilled work. Given those limitations, are there jobs at a light level of exertion in the national economy this person can perform?"

Let's simplify this hypothetical by breaking it down into its parts using references and definitions from the *Dictionary of Occupational Titles.*

1) Sitting = 6 hours/Standing and walking = 6 hours and lifting 20 pounds occasionally/10 pounds frequently. This is the definition of light work (You may wish to review the definitions given in The Appendix). Under these limitations this person would also be able to perform sedentary work as well but the ALJ has asked only for light jobs.

2) Frequent fingering and handling mean one could perform work activity that required fine and gross manipulation up to 2/3 of the time, spread throughout the workday, but not work that requires fingering and handling on a constant basis. (Frequent fingering and feeling would preclude many, but not all, production jobs).

3) Avoid extreme heat, humidity and respiratory irritants means that you'll probably be looking for jobs that are performed indoors instead of jobs such as an unarmed security guard who may need to regularly walk the perimeter of a building property on hot and cold days or a gate guard who may be exposed to diesel truck fumes.

4) Occasional interaction with the public means that this person can be exposed to the general public for only 1/3 of a workday. You want to avoid positions like customer service, cashier, sales attendant, or ticket taker which have frequent or constant interaction with the public.

5) Routine, repetitive, unskilled work means that all the work that

would fit into this hypothetical will be unskilled work with a Significant Vocational Preparation (SVP) of 1 or 2 and the job tasks can be learned and performed adequately within 30 days or less. Some semi-skilled jobs at a level SVP-3 that take one to three months to learn the job and perform the work adequately may be permissible to some judges as these jobs are unskilled at entry level.

Are there jobs which could be performed within these limitations? The jobs would have to be light in exertion and performed in a relatively protected work environment, The postural limitations are consistent with light work so the ability to climb, balance, stoop, kneel, crouch, and crawl on an occasional basis would not significantly limit the performance of most light jobs. This person would need to have a job that did not require contact with the general public more than a third of the day with that time not concentrated but spread out over a workday, and the work would need to be unskilled.

In all likelihood, there are jobs in the national economy that this hypothetical person could perform? Within these limitations most other VE's would be able to find work this person could do. Examples might be light house cleaning or inspecting and packager in a factory.

Suggestions for Responding to Hypothetical Questions: Our View

From time to time vocational experts ask what advice we would give to rehabilitation counselors and others wishing to become vocational experts. We thought that a good way to end our discussion of hypothetical questions was to ask several persons we considered experts to list some tips or pointers they considered important advice in responding to hypothetical questions from an Administrative Law Judge. Here, in no particular order, are some tips a vocational expert will do well to remember:

a. **The ALJ Makes the Decision**. The vocational expert is in the hearing to provide information on vocational issues requested by the judge. Most of this information is provided in responses to hypothetical questions. Hypothetical questions are designed to provide input to help the judge make the disability decision. Understanding that the judge makes the decision prevents the expert from role confusion, like responding to questions, such as medical questions, questions which lie outside of the vocational expert's professional field.

b. **The Hearing is about the Claimant, Not About You**. With the tension of a disability hearing, listening to the testimony of others, and sorting through all of the information before you, there is the tendency to lose your perspective and think more of your role and the responses you will provide. One way to keep your focus and the right perspective is to consciously say to yourself "this is the claimant's hearing".

c. **Listen to Each Word of the Hypothetical and Respond Only to the Content of the Hypothetical Question**. It is natural, particularly at the beginning, for vocational experts to feel they are "under the gun", so to speak, and for the VE to either anticipate what they think the judge is going to say; or, feeling pressure, miss some of the content within the hypothetical. Always ask the judge to repeat the hypothetical or any part of the hypothetical you think you may have missed.

d. **Function is Everything**. Attorneys and claimants are not always well-versed in how to phrase questions to vocational experts in functional terms. As a VE you cannot provide a response to questions unless the question is placed in terms of function, i.e., what a person can or cannot do. When questions are asked calling for a subjective answer, it is imperative to ask the person to rephrase the question in functional terms.

e. **The Job is Not About Numbers, but the Numbers Need to be Accurate**. So much emphasis seems to be directed toward providing statistical information. There is the tendency to think that the whole job is giving numbers to the judge. Providing accurate statistics is important, but vocational experts cannot narrow their perspective and allow themselves to settle into such a reduced role. Most judges look upon vocational experts as experts in their professional field. Should we expect less of ours?

Naming Jobs a Claimant Can Perform

To review some of the main points from our discussion about hypothetical questions, the purpose of the hypothetical format is to present alternative work options to help the administrative law judge make a determination whether or not the person seeking disability payments is able to make a vocational adjustment to other work that exists in the national economy. The hypothetical type of questioning leaves the burden of interpreting the medical evidence to the Administrative Law Judge. This type of questioning comes at Step 5 in the decision-making process. Presumably, by this stage in the 5-step process the ALJ has reached a decision at Step 4 that the claimant cannot do his/her past work.

Each hypothetical situation begins by assuming a "hypothetical" person with the same vocational profile -- age, educational and work experience -- as the claimant in the hearing. The vocational profile is then followed by having the VE assume a set, maybe several sets, of functional limitations which are just possibilities and naming jobs the person can perform within each set of limitations. Only if the ALJ accepts a set of limitations as accurately portraying the vocational abilities of a claimant does a situation become part of the hearing decision.

After presenting each set of limitations, the ALJ will ask if there are any jobs the expert can name that this person would be able to perform. The concluding statement of the hypothetical goes something like this: "considering a person with this vocational profile and these limitations in function, are there jobs in the national economy you can name that this person can perform".

If a vocational expert believes there are jobs this hypothetical person can perform within the limitations given by the ALJ, the VE will name the jobs in a statement like this: "Your honor, given these limitations and the vocational profile of this hypothetical person presented earlier, it is my opinion this person could perform the following jobs". The VE would then proceed to name the jobs. If, on the other hand, the VE believes that the person cannot perform any jobs under the limitations, the response to the hypothetical question is that there are no jobs: the response would be stated like this: "in my opinion there are no jobs that a person can perform on a sustained basis within those limitations".

For example, let's consider this situation: the judge asked the VE to use the profile of a former construction laborer who is 53 years old with a high school education, and complaints about a chronic back problem. The hypothetical posed to the VE would be:

ALJ: "Please assume a person with the same work background as the claimant and that I find from the evidence that this hypothetical person can stand and/or walk for approximately 6 hours in an 8-hour day, and lift no more than 20 pounds at a time with frequent lifting or carrying of objects weighing up to 10 pounds. Would he be able to engage in his past work or, if not, could he engage in any other work?" The VE would respond

VE: "Under these limitations, the worker would not be able to perform his past work which was very heavy in exertion. This person would be reduced to light and sedentary work."

If the Administrative Law Judge considered light work to be a possible option for alternative work, the judge would likely ask the VE to name a representative number of jobs the expert believes this hypothetical person could perform within these limitations. A representative number of jobs provided by the VE usually range from two (2) to six (6) with three examples being the number most often requested by the ALJ in disability hearings.. Questioning would continue:

ALJ: "Further assume if the hypothetical person could not perform his past work under those limitations, are there other light jobs this person could perform given the same vocational profile and those same set of limitations?"

VE: "In my opinion there would be a range of light work a person with this vocational profile could perform. This person could work as a cafeteria attendant, a maid or house person in a motel or hotel, and a parking lot attendant. In the national economy there are 120,000 thousand cafeteria attendants. The DOT reference for this occupation is 311.677-010. In the national economy, there are over 90,000 maids and house persons that work in hotels or motels. The DOT reference for this occupation is 323.687-014. And, in the national economy there are over 26,000 parking lot attendants. The DOT reference for this occupation is 915.473-010. The DOT lists these jobs as light in exertion and unskilled with an SVP of 2". These jobs are only representative of the light jobs in the national economy this person could perform. (Notice, the VE did not cite jobs in the state or local economy. The reason for this is that the SSI and SSDI programs require listing jobs in the national economy only).

In her presentation titled "Social Security Vocational Expert Most Common Hypotheticals" at the International Association of Rehabilitation Professionals Conference in Puerto Rico in 2012, Dr. Amy Vercillo (13) posed questions similar to those below to a group of vocational experts and asked if, given those situations, they would be able to locate jobs. There is a surprising variation among the responses, showing how different various experts view work in the national economy. At least some experts were able to find jobs under each set of limitations.

1.   If the hypothetical includes a person who requires a range of work at a light level of exertion with the need for a sit/stand option meaning the employee would need to sit for several minutes during each hour of work, would there be jobs available?

Yes (94%)

No (5%)

2.   If a hypothetical includes a person who requires a range of work at the sedentary level of exertion with the need for a sit/stand option, meaning the person would need to stand for a few minutes during each hour of work, would there be jobs available?

Yes (90%)

No (9%)

3.   Are there jobs available if an employee can use his/her non-dominant hand only occasionally (1/3 of the day) if they are also reduced to work at a light level of exertion?

Yes (83%)

No (16%)

4.   If an employee can use the non-dominant hand only occasionally and was further reduced to work at a sedentary level of exertion, are there jobs that exist?

Yes (49%)

No (50%)

5.   If an employee can perform work at the light level of exertion, but could only use their dominant hand occasionally, are there jobs?

Yes (61%)

No (38%)

6.   Are there jobs at the sedentary work level if an employee has the use of the dominant hand only occasionally?

Yes (30%)

No (69%)

7.   Are there jobs at a light level of exertion available for non-English speakers?

Yes (95%)

No (4%)

8.   If a person is restricted to a light level of exertion but cannot work with the public, would there be any jobs he/she could do?

Yes (95%)

No (5%)

9.   If an employee working at the light exertion level found it necessary to elevate his/her legs to 12" occasionally (up to 1/3 of the day) would work be available?

Yes (43%)

No (57%)

10.   If an employee is restricted to the sedentary level of exertion and needed to elevate his/her legs at a height of 12" occasionally (1/3 of the day) would work be available?

Yes (74%)

No (26%)

11.   If an individual requires more than occasional supervision on a sustained basis, would he/she be able to engage in substantial gainful employment?

Yes (13%)

No (87%)

12.   Are there jobs available for a hypothetical person at any level of exertion who is unable to work with co-workers in work-

related tasks (no tandem work) but would be able to work in proximity to other workers?

Yes (77%)

No (23%)

Some vocational experts feel that an ALJ expects them to find jobs and they become frustrated when the job base they understand becomes so eroded that there are very few jobs in significant numbers located in the national or local economy. The vocational expert needs to remember several things in reference to presenting statistical information, such as the numbers of jobs, to the court:

(1) The ALJ, not the vocational expert, determines whether or not jobs exist in significant numbers. The expert needs to provide the numbers given in the source material and let the judge decide the relevance of the numbers;

(2) The vocational expert must present the information truthfully and accurately to the court. The VE has taken an oath to tell the truth and in presenting information to the court the VE needs to be as accurate as possible and true to his/her source material; and, finally,

(3) Remember,rthe VE is the expert on vocational matters for this case. But experts are expected to stay within their role, providing vocational guidance and information based upon their knowledge and experience to help improve the quality of the decision the ALJ has to make.

Jobs in the National Economy

In the illustration, given above, the VE was asked by the ALJ if the hypothetical person could not perform his past work under the limitations provided, are there other jobs this person could perform given the same vocational profile and those same limitations?" To this question the VE responded with the names of three occupations the hypothetical person with the same vocational profile and the same functional limitations as the claimant would be able to perform. These occupations were Cafeteria Attendant, a Parking Lot Attendant, and Maid/House Person. After naming jobs the VE listed the DOT reference for those occupations and the national number of those jobs in the national economy.

Where do these job numbers come from? In the past vocational experts relied upon a number of data sources. There were businesses set up to analyze data and extrapolate information from a variety of government and private resources and provide vocational experts with job numbers especially for the purpose of testifying in disability hearings. But the primary resource for job information has always been research provided by the United States Department of Labor.

Today, most vocational experts use computerized programs as the main source of their information. These computer programs rely heavily upon information from the Department of Labor also. For instance, SkillTRAN and Occubrowse say that their primary source for the job numbers they report come from the Occupational Employment Survey (OES), data collected directly from employer survey responses. OES statistics are widely recognized as the most immediate and accurate source for the numbers of jobs in the United States today because the Survey is taken from sources closest to the actual jobs and updated annually.

Cross Examination of the Vocational Expert

During the testimony of the vocational expert, the Administrative Law Judge examines several possible outcomes and through using hypothetical questions presented to the VE, the judge gains support for the option which is ultimately chosen. As one ALJ put it "at Step 5 the testimony of the VE is critical to the information the ALJ needs to resolve the case".

At the conclusion of the VE testimony in response to the judge's hypothetical questions, the ALJ asks the claimant or the claimant's representative if they have any questions to ask the vocational expert. Cross examination of the vocational expert is usually the last part of the hearing.

Cross examination of the VE on behalf of the claimant is intended to strengthen the case for the position that the claimant can no longer perform full-time competitive work. Generally, the way a claimant or a claimant's representative begins his/her cross examination of the vocational expert is by adding additional limitations to the hypothetical questions the ALJ has already asked.

Some of the additional limitations may reinforce statements made by the claimant during the testimony; some may emphasize information brought out in testimony during the hearing; some questions may take note of new evidence not explored in the hearing; some of these questions may draw attention to medical source statements from treating or non-treating sources, and some questions may concern the jobs the VE has named during the series of hypothetical questions.

At Step 5 in order for the Administrative Law Judge to deny benefits, the Social Security Administration must show that a claimant can perform full time, competitive work on a sustained basis. That is, the claimant must be able to work 40 hours a week, 8 hours a day. For this reason, some of the questioning during cross examination will likely try to show that the claimant cannot work full time or complete a full workday or work week. One strategy attorneys use to demonstrate their claimant cannot perform full time work is to direct questions to the VE during cross examination concerning a hypothetical person taking time off task beyond the normal breaks and exceeding the normal absences from work because of medical or psychological reasons. The example below shows ways a claimant representative in his/her cross examination of the vocational expert may use off task and absences to show that their client cannot perform full-time work.

Attorney: "In the hearing today the Judge asked you to consider an individual of the claimant's age, education, and work experience who could do light work and you suggested this person could do full time work as a maid in a hotel, a parking lot attendant, and a cafeteria attendant. If that person had to take additional breaks that added up to his being off task and away from the job more than 20% of the day beyond the normal breaks, would this person be able to work"?

VE: "No, under that limitation the person would not be able to perform full-time work. 20% exceeds the normal tolerance for being off task during the workday and I believe the person would not be able to sustain work under that additional limitation".

Seldom are the questions asked by the claimant's attorney meant to embarrass the expert or attack the expert personally. However, an attorney has the legal obligation to provide their claimant the best possible advocacy and if flaws or inconsistencies exist in the VE testimony, the expert can expect an attorney to exploit those weaknesses on behalf of the claimant. To avoid conflict of this kind, experts are expected to be present during the hearing or by telephone, listen to all the testimony, and use the most reliable information sources possible for their vocational testimony (See the earlier section on Numbers for the Jobs in the National Economy).

Finally, for the vocational expert to respond to the questions in cross examination, the limitations provided during cross examination must be placed in functional terminology. That is, the questions must be framed in such a way as to show how a limitation would affect that person's ability to function on the job. The two examples below demonstrate how questions may be placed in functional terms: Continuing with the line of questioning to the VE Joshua Stein:

Attorney: "in the hearing today my client says that she has to elevate her legs three times a day for 30 minutes at a time to relieve the swelling and numbness in her feet caused by her diabetes. Would she be able to perform the jobs you have named as a maid, a laundry aide, or a cafeteria attendant if she had to elevate her legs three times a day for 30 minutes"?

VE: "The amount of time needed to elevate her legs would have to be confined to the allowable breaks provided during the day. If the person had to elevate their legs three times a day for 30 minutes outside of the normal breaks, the time away from the job would exceed the amount of allowable time off task during a workday. My opinion is that anything more that 10% to 12% of time off task beyond the normal breaks would exceed the normal tolerance for an employee being off task during a workday. For example, the XZ elevation of one's legs in the workplace, in my experience, is not an accommodation most employers are willing to provide".

Attorney, "Finally, can a person perform the jobs you have named if they have to be absent four times a month."

VE: "I do not believe that a person who has to miss work four times a month can sustain full-time work without special accommodation. In my experience the normal allowable absences in most structured jobs is one day a month".

Functional Limitations and Work Options to Consider When Addressing Specific Limitations in Function

Below are typical situations vocational experts are asked to address in their testimony. As we have seen, a situation may be presented to the vocational expert in the form of a hypothetical question from the administrative law judge. Or a situation may be presented to the vocational expert as part of the cross examination from a claimant or claimant's attorney. These situations generally arise from what has gone on during court proceedings, and each of these situations concern limitations in function that affect a person's ability to perform full time competitive work.

The following situations showing limitation in function regularly come about in the hearings. Our attempt here is to highlight a number of functional limitations which regularly come up in disability hearings, show how VE's may analyze and respond to them, and present some possible work options. The responses provided in this book are just suggestions, the opinions of only a few vocational experts. The responses do not represent the collective opinions of vocational experts. The responses provided are meant only to show the ways vocational experts analyze questions presented to them and respond to an ALJ"s inquiry during the fact-finding phase of the hearing, or to questions during cross examination from a claimant's representative.

1. **How many unscheduled breaks are typically allowed in a workday?**

Daily work breaks in most structured jobs are scheduled at approximately two-hour intervals. There is usually a break in the morning of approximately 15 minutes and another break in the afternoon of about 15 minutes with a 30-minute break for lunch, making up about 12 ½ % of an 8-hour day. Except for occasional restroom breaks, employers do not typically allow for excessive work recesses outside of the normal work schedule. There is no standard for the number of extra breaks allowed, but extra, unscheduled breaks could easily exceed the normal tolerance for time away from the workstation and impact job performance. This question could easily fall under the rubric of "off-task" behavior (see below). The current census in the professional field is that anything over 10% to 12% that a worker has to be off task from the job beyond the normal breaks would preclude competitive work.

2. **If an employee is off task more than 20% of the workday, would any full-time competitive work be available?**

Research is scant on the subject. In its policy manual one manufacturer we found has stated that anything over 2-3 % beyond the allowed breaks exceeds the normal tolerances for being off-task and away from the workstation. The job involved working on a production line. The present census among professionals in the field indicate that anything over 10% to 12% beyond the normal breaks would preclude competitive work. Therefore, most vocational experts, we believe, would consider 20% of the workday off-task to exceed the normal tolerances. Our opinion is that most employers would say that they would not be willing to pay an employee a full day's wage for less than six hours of work. This is especially true for unskilled work which, by its very nature, is less flexible with few workplace accommodations.

3. Claimant's That "Can't Be Around Other People"

One of the most common complaints we hear from claimants in the courtroom today is "I can't be around people" and "I can't be in crowds". In many cases their disability has caused them to retreat from their friends and family and this behavior has become a factor in their inability to work. Most VE's would consider this behavior as a mental and emotional condition, a symptom of depression. But is this a situational depression which may well improve if the person becomes more active; or, is it part of a more serious condition, such as major depression? This is what the ALJ must figure out.

For part of the answer to this question, the Administrative Law Judge turns to the VE to determine how this behavior may affect a person's ability to work; and, that if there are jobs, what kind of jobs may be available. Typically, the ALJ will ask for simple, unskilled work because detailed and complex tasks may be too taxing for a person with this condition. Moreover, the hypothetical will likely include jobs with little or no contact with the public or co-workers, and little interaction with supervisors.

There are unskilled jobs involving little or no contact with the public, co-workers or limited interaction with supervisors? Such jobs include cleaning positions, whether at home, a hotel, or a cleaning job at a manufacturing plant. If, on the other hand, the ALJ asks for jobs with no contact with the public, co-workers, or supervisors, would there be jobs? The base of jobs would likely be eroded substantially if a person cannot have contact with the public or co-workers, but some cleaning jobs, and some production jobs with no tandem tasks would likely remain. Unskilled jobs with no supervision are unlikely, however. You may develop your own ideas, but our thinking is that no competitive jobs exist in a vacuum. There are no unskilled competitive jobs that exist, we feel, which can accommodate no interaction with supervisors.

4. **Would the use of an assistive device, like a walker or a cane, have any impact upon sedentary work?**

Many sedentary jobs can still be performed if an employee needs to use an assistive device to ambulate to and from the workstation as they will be seated for most of the workday. Under those circumstances the use of such a device would not be a work accommodation. The limitation of having to use a cane when walking would not significantly reduce the occupational base for most sedentary jobs. Unskilled jobs such as an information clerk or a sedentary cashier are examples of jobs that could still be done under this limitation.

However, if such an ambulatory device, like a cane, is needed for balance, as well as ambulation, it is likely that the vocational expert would not be able to find jobs a claimant could perform. The rationale is that if an employee needs extensive use of both legs and arms to move from place to place, then the person would not be able to hold and carry even light objects, such as office supplies. If an assistive device is needed for balance, the adjudicator will likely follow the guidance provided in publication SSR 96-9p that says "the occupational base for an individual who must use such a device for balance because of significant involvement of both lower extremities (e.g., because of a neurological impairment) may be significantly eroded". Finally, if a person needed a cane for balance, even simple movement would create additional time off task.

An employee needing to use a walker or scooter in the workplace would have to receive special permission from an employer. Ambulatory devices of this type are not regular options available to all employees; the employee needing to use a walker or scooter would need a special work accommodation from that employer.

5. **Can the jobs you named be performed if this person has only a 6th grade education?**

Our belief is that possessing only a marginal education will not preclude competitive employment. Many jobs require only a short demonstration instead of written instructions to learn the job and have no additional reading and writing requirement. Such jobs would include cleaners, particularly night cleaners and housekeepers, assemblers, and many other unskilled factory jobs. However, the vocational expert may need to examine other aspects of the job requirements before making the determination a person can perform the job with a marginal education.

6. **If an employee needs more than occasional supervision, would substantial gainful employment be available to that person?**

Some jobs involve more supervision than others. In some jobs the employee is able to perform the job tasks with relatively little contact with supervisors. An example might be a maid working in a hotel or motel. For this question, the aim of the claimant representative is usually to point out that the claimant would need more supervision than the average employee would be allowed in a competitive employment environment. Even if the supervisor works near the employee, s/he will not be able to provide extra supervision that detracts from his or her own work responsibilities. A need for supervision for over 1/3 of the workday would be more consistent with non-competitive work, such as a sheltered workshop.

7. **If an employee can have only occasional contact with the public, co-workers, or supervisors, what effect would that have upon the jobs which you have named?**

The question usually is meant to emphasize psychological limitations that can be exacerbated when a person has to work around other people. Jobs like customer service, sales attendant, and rental clerks require more than occasional contact with the public, while cleaning jobs, laundry jobs (sorting and folding), and production jobs, like assembly and inspecting, usually do not. Normally jobs which require tandem or coordinated tasks (some production jobs) require more than occasional contact with co-workers. There are almost no unskilled or semi-skilled jobs that do not require at least a modicum of supervisory interaction. However, there are some jobs, such as a housekeeper in a motel or hotel and a laundry aide that usually require only occasional contact with a supervisor.

8. **If an employee had no use of his/her non-dominant arm, how would that affect the ability to perform the jobs you have cited?**

The loss of the ability to use the non-dominant hand, alone, will not preclude competitive employment. The ruling in the case of Odle v. Secretary of Health and Human Services (found in SSR 87-11c), the court decided that "the loss of, or the loss of the use of, an arm or hand is not disabling per se, since prior court decisions have held that an individual who has lost the use of an arm or hand can still engage in substantial gainful activity," even when the claimant had a limited education.

The *Selected Characteristics of Occupations* from the Department of Labor does not address the frequency of fine or gross manipulation for each limb individually. This is where the insight of a vocational expert will help the court better understand which jobs can be performed within the given limitations. Production jobs and sedentary jobs would be counter-indicated because most require frequent use of both hands. Possible examples of jobs that could accommodate those limitations might be an usher or a gate guard. Generally, experts would respond that there would be no jobs if the person had no use or limited use of the dominant hand.

9. Do the sedentary positions you have named allow for an employee to stand up and stretch as long as they remain at the workstation? (sit/stand option)

A sitting and standing option normally applies to sedentary work in which an employee can perform the work in either a standing or sitting position. Most sedentary positions will allow an employee to stand up and stretch (sometimes called a "sit/stand option") during the workday as long as the employee remains at their workstation.

If this question is part of a hypothetical from the judge, then often the claimant's representative may add an additional limitation that would eliminate any jobs you may have offered in response to this question.

Should the vocational expert name jobs in response to a hypothetical question which includes a sit/stand option, a typical follow-up question from an attorney or non-attorney may go something like this: "If, in addition to standing and stretching, an employee would need to walk away from the work station for several minutes every half hour to relieve pain, how would this affect the sedentary occupational base?"

This question may best be addressed with a discussion of the amount of time a worker can be off-task and unproductive. Let's unpack this additional limitation. If there are 16 half hours in a workday and an employee needs to leave the workstation for even 3-5 minutes each half hour then that would total 48-80 minutes in total that s/he would not be performing their job tasks. If 3-5 minutes is beyond the normal breaks, that amount of time off task would stretch or exceed the limits, 10% to 12%, of allowable time a person can be off task. That loss of time represents a significant loss of productivity.

Some judges have asked if there are jobs at a light level of exertion which provide a sitting or standing option. This question seems contrary to the very definition of the term. However, some judges and some VE's reason that there are jobs listed in the *Dictionary of Occupational Titles* that are performed at a light level of exertion where an employee can sit or stand **at will** without significant loss of productivity. Such jobs may include cafeteria cashiers, toll collectors, some parking lot attendants, change booth cashiers, and some bench assemblers. In naming these jobs the VE may need to reduce the number of jobs available for jobs like bench assembler and parking lot attendant and note that naming of these jobs is based upon the VE's professional judgment as to how these jobs are generally performed.

10. If an employee can perform only occasional fine or gross manipulation, how would that affect that person's ability to work?

Fine manipulation requires the use of the fingers to manipulate small objects, such as writing instruments or operating a keyboard. Gross manipulation means handling, grasping or holding objects inside the hand. Restricted fine and gross manipulation will erode any occupational base to some degree, but jobs will likely remain at all levels of exertion.

Jobs in the light range will be the most numerous. Jobs in the medium to very heavy category may not require much fine manipulation but almost always require frequent to constant gross manipulation. But contrary to general opinion, the *Dictionary of Occupational Titles* list many production jobs that require only frequent use of the hands for reaching, handling, and feeling. These include some assembling, inspection, and packaging jobs.

The sedentary occupational base is different, though. If an employee will be seated for most of the day, then s/he will need to have at least frequent use of the hands. This is especially true of unskilled occupations. This opinion is in a closely adhered to and frequently cited passage from SSR 96-9p "Most unskilled sedentary jobs require good use of both hands and the fingers.

Any significant manipulative limitation of an individual's ability to handle and work with small objects with both hands will result in a significant erosion of the unskilled sedentary occupational base."

11. If an employee can only stand or walk for four hours in an 8-hour day, can that person perform light work?

This limitation falls between the light and sedentary range of work with the lifting and carrying falling in the light range and the standing and walking in the sedentary range. Under this limitation the sedentary occupations appropriate for a claimant would remain within the person's residual functional capacity (RFC).

But would light work be available? SSR 83-19 states that "the full range of light work requires standing or walking, off and on, for a total of approximately 6 hours in an 8-hour day". Indeed, many jobs at the light level of exertion require employees to stand and walk for the entire shift. Moreover, in order to be consistent with the *Dictionary of Occupational Titles*, the Disability Determination Section in their analysis, found in the A section of the case record under Disability Explanation, will always limit a person to the sedentary range of exertion when that person has been found to be able to walk and stand only four hours in an 8-hour day.

Some vocational experts adhere strictly to the definitions in the regulations and testify that if the person cannot stand and walk at least 6 hours in an 8-hour day, that person cannot perform light work. On the other hand, other VE's argue that an RFC of light allows for a range of what is often called "modified light work". They argue that, based upon their experience in working in job placement with persons having disabilities, a percentage of jobs listed as light in the *Dictionary of Occupational Titles* actually can be performed with a limitation of standing and walking no more than 4 hours in an 8-hour day. Typically cited are cashiers in small retail shops, cafeterias, or convenience stores and gate guards.

When naming these jobs, VE's would generally reduce the national statistics. The percentage of "modified light" positions may be a small fraction of all positions under the DOT code; however, even if only a reduced percentage of jobs can be performed within the RFC, it may still yield a significant number of jobs because these jobs in these occupations are so numerous.

The VE needs to remember that modified light work is not consistent with the DOT and at the end of the hearing when the ALJ asks if the testimony is consistent with the DOT, the VE needs to point out this discrepancy and explain that the response to modified work is based upon professional experience in his/her chosen field.

12. Transferable Skills for Persons 50 or Over:

Following your classification of jobs during a hearing, an ALJ may ask you if there are skills from a claimant's past work which will transfer to other jobs in the national economy. From your counseling experience in helping clients find jobs, your planned response may cause you to consider such things as human traits like honesty and integrity or life skills, things learned from a hobby or doing part-time jobs on weekends. These skills may be useful in finding jobs for clients, but they are not as helpful in disability hearings. For SSA purposes transferable skills do not include soft skills such as social skills, a strong work ethic, or traits such as punctuality.

For the Social Security disability programs, SSI and SSDI, transferable skills are narrowly defined in the regulations governing the disability program and have a very different meaning from the use of the term in the job exploration field. Under SSA regulations transferable skills only become an issue if the claimant is over 50 years old. Even then, taking the regulations into account, there are other conditions the ALJ and vocational experts must consider: (1)

After a claimant has turned 50, the agency will grant benefits if the claimant is limited to sedentary work and has no past work at the sedentary level to which they can return and no work skills that transfer to any sedentary work. (2) At age 55, the SSA sets a similar standard but the claimant must either have past work at the light or sedentary exertional level to which they can return or have transferable skills to jobs at a light level of exertion. If not, benefits are awarded. (3) At age 60 the bar is raised and the claimant must be able to perform work at the medium level of exertion.

There are a few technical details VE's need to know about transferable skills as well. You may consider these reminders common sense but as you no doubt know, there is nothing more uncommon in this world than common sense. Skills are only transferable from skilled or semi-skilled work. Skills do not transfer to or from unskilled work of SVP 1 or 2. Skills cannot be transferred to a higher skill or a higher level of exertion. For example, skills from a licensed practical nurse would not transfer to a registered nurse because a registered nurse is an SVP 7 whereas a licensed practical nurse is an SVP 6. Although some of the skills a security officer knows would be helpful to a police officer, these skills would not transfer because skills from a job at the light exertional level are not transferable to a job at the medium exertional level or higher.

The ALJ asking you these questions is only concerned with skills that provide direct transfer into another job with little or no additional vocational training. The skills of a Certified Nursing Assistant would in all probability transfer to the position of a Companion. In the open job market, as we know, CNA's are much in demand by employers in the home care business. On the other hand, the skills of a retail manager do not readily transfer to a clerical job like a receptionist. A retail manager may perform some data entry, typing and interacting with customers by phone, but the skills of a retail manager would not transfer to the job of a receptionist. To become a receptionist would require additional training.

Clerical skills are some of the most easily transferable skills to other jobs because those skills will be used in nearly the same fashion across all professions, whether it's a secretary at a school, an insurance agency or an accounting firm. But the VE needs to be careful to remember the skills must cover the complete job with no additional training required.

Jobs as salespersons generally don't transfer into other sales positions unless they are selling the same products or services. The skills of an automobile salesperson would not transfer into a job as a food sales representative. Skills in the sales field are mostly in product knowledge not in the approach to customers. Nursing skills tend to remain the same whether the nurse is in a private home, a hospital or a clinic. A registered nurse would likely have transferable skills to most other nursing specialties at a lower skill or level of exertion.

There is still wide variation in what VE's are to consider transferable skills. Some vocational experts who have worked extensively in job placement may supplement the regulations with their own professional knowledge. Other vocational experts will rely on occupational group arrangements (first 3 numbers in the D.O.T. code) in conjunction with work fields, and the Guide for Occupational Exploration (GOE) by the US Employment Service. The GOE codes correspond to jobs with similar interests and aptitudes. Many vocational expert witnesses also use Work Fields (WF), Materials, Products, Subject Matter, and Services (MPSMS), and worker traits. But whatever approach you take, you need to blend your knowledge with the meanings and regulatory advice provided by the Social Security Administration.

The concept of transferable skills has changed in the last several decades as America has moved from an industrial to a services economy. This change has reduced both the number of occupations having transferable skills as well as their usefulness. In job placement today, the research tells us, traits are more valuable to potential employers than transferable skills. But this is not true in a disability hearing for SSA. The best advice for VE's seems to be to stay as closely as possible within the meaning of the SSA regulations.

13. If an employee has problems with their vision, at what point would they be unable to work?

Questions that contain visual limitations in a disability hearing are rare. But just when you think you don't need to know about how a visual limitation affects a person's ability to perform their past work or alternative work, a visual limitation comes bedded in the ALJ's hypothetical.

Visual limitations vary among claimants and present themselves in varying ways. On occasion the administrative law judge must come to a conclusion as to what effect a reduction in vision has upon a claimant's ability to work and determine at what point reduced vision prevents a person from performing full time, competitive activity.

Certain medical conditions often lie at the root of diminished visual perception. One of the more common causes of visual problems may be a complication of diabetes. This is very frequently listed in the disability report. Diabetic retinopathy can potentially result in blindness. Early symptoms usually include blurred vision or dark spots. Multiple Sclerosis can cause double vision (diplopia). Traumatic brain injuries can cause retinal detachment. Usher syndrome can cause myopia (tunnel vision) as well as photosensitivity. Since claimants may not list all the limitations in the record, it may be helpful to familiarize yourself with the myriad diseases that have the potential to cause visual disturbances.

The Department of Labor in the *Selected Characteristics of Occupations* has analyzed and rated the visual requirements for each job in the *Dictionary of Occupational Titles.* The list below provides the criteria job analysts for the Department of Labor use to measure the visual requirements for each job. If you are using a computer program, such as SkillTran, you can find the visual requirements for each job under the section titled "physical demands".

NE - Near Acuity - Visual clarity measured at 20′

FA - Far Acuity - Clarity of vision past 20 feet.

DE - Depth Perception - Three-dimensional vision and the ability to judge dimension and spatial relation

AC – Accommodation – The ability of the eye to bring things into focus

CV - Color Vision – The ability to identify and distinguish colors

FV - Field of Vision – The totality of what the eye can see when in a fixed position

Near visual acuity is a <u>frequent</u> requirement for most jobs. For claimants who have limitations with their near vision, jobs that require close attention to detail, such as jobs with clerical responsibilities like data entry or production jobs like assembly of small products may not be appropriate. Jobs that require driving would also be a concern for claimants with limitations in near visual acuity.

It would be difficult for a claimant with significant near acuity limitations to return to work that required frequent reading or data entry such as a secretary, hotel front desk clerks, and teachers. Depending upon how severe the limitation is, other work that requires <u>none</u> to <u>occasional</u> near acuity may be appropriate. A Job like a bus person or dishwasher comes to mind. **Far acuity** affects fewer jobs. However, a person with a job such as a parking lot attendant or an usher may have difficulty performing essential work functions with a severe limitation in their ability to see for longer distances.

Colorblindness won't affect the performance in most jobs and is usually not an issue in a person's returning to work. Jobs that require occasional or frequent ability to distinguish between colors can affect certain jobs where an employee is required to sort or distinguish by color, such as laundry sorters or those that work in a plant nursery.

If a claimant's colorblindness is congenital, they will likely have already adjusted to their limitations and chosen past work that does not require color vision. However, if the claimant has acquired colorblindness through conditions such as retinal or optic nerve damage past work may be precluded. So be prepared with possibilities for other work that does not require color vision for the main functions of the job.

Depth perception allows us to determine the distance between objects. Depth perception requires binocular vision. Claimants with vision in only one eye will have diminished depth perception. But, in most cases, a person can rely on other visual clues such as shading, size familiarity and occlusion to compensate for the loss of vision in one eye. A claimant with vision in just one eye may be able to perform a range of jobs that do not require frequent to constant depth perception. Such jobs may include mail clerks, laundry workers and office helpers. Jobs that require frequent depth perception or where lack of depth perception would cause hazards, like truck drivers, would not be appropriate. Helpful resources are the *Revised Handbook of Analyzing jobs* (RHAJ) and the *Selected Characteristics of Occupations* (SCO).

14. **Are there jobs that this person can do with a loss of hearing.**

Problems with hearing loss as a primary, severe impairment are relatively rare at the appeals level of the Social Security Administration. If a hearing condition is disabling, the problem most likely meets the listings and the claimant would be declared disabled at Step 3 But hypothetical questions are presented to the vocational expert from time to time as conditions that contribute to the disabling condition; and, the vocational expert needs to be prepared to address hearing loss in their responses.

Unless the claimant meets a medical listing for hearing loss at Step 3, the hearing loss will not typically preclude all jobs. There should be jobs this person can do if only the hearing loss is considered. When coupled with other physical or psychological problems, the combined limitation will likely shape the kind of work a person can do or reduce the numbers of jobs within the occupations the VE is considering.

For instance, hearing loss will almost always affect, and, depending upon the degree of hearing loss, even eliminate from consideration jobs that require the use of a telephone, jobs that require public interaction, or jobs that require interaction with co-workers, particular where there are tandem tasks involved. If other severe problems are present, such as anxiety or depressions, the combined effect may well preclude work altogether.

In selecting jobs that a person can do with a hearing loss, the VE will also need to consider that most of the claimants with hearing loss acquired the condition well into their life rather than having loss of hearing as a congenital condition during their formative years. As a result, this person will not likely have familiarity with sign language, further limiting their ability to communicate effectively.

What kinds of jobs are appropriate for persons with severe hearing loss? One VE had an interesting perspective on this subject. She said the jobs that persons with severe hearing loss can perform are similar, if not identical, to jobs performed by employees who cannot speak the native language. This seems to be a good way of approaching this subject. When asked for jobs a person with a hearing loss can perform, the VE may turn to those jobs normally performed by persons who cannot communicate verbally.

Types of jobs that can be performed by non-native language speakers include those in the cleaning industry. These types of jobs can be hotel housekeepers, residential housekeepers, office cleaners, industrial cleaners, janitors, etc. Other jobs that have traditionally been able to support workers who do not communicate verbally include dishwashers, some assembly work that doesn't require organization or tandem tasks between coworkers to complete the job, such as hand packagers, sewing machine operators, and laundry workers.

In searching for examples of jobs that a limitation of severe hearing loss might impede would, quite naturally, include those jobs that involved frequent communication with the public or coworkers. This would include most, but not all, clerical or office jobs. Excluded would be clerical work that requires an employee to screen phone calls, take payments or directly interacts with the public. But not all clerical work would be precluded. Jobs, such as an office helper, bookkeepers or data entry clerks do not require public interaction and, depending upon the industry, little communication with coworkers. Some of these jobs, like office helper, may well fall into the unskilled and category which most judges hope the VE can identify.

Appendix

Vocational Factors

Years ago, in the formation of its disability program, the Social Security Administration recognized wisely that the three most important vocational factors affecting a person's residual functional capacity and their ability to work were the combination of a person's age, their education, and their work experience. The wisdom of using these three factors to make a determination has withstood the test of time. Age, education, and work experience are the three (3) key vocational factors that go into making up a person's vocational profile. Vocational Experts use a combination of these same three factors in making an assessment of their client's ability to work and identifying the kinds of jobs that person is likely to be able to perform within their residual functional capacity.

Factor # 1: Age, and the Ability to Adjust to Alternative Work

"Age" refers to an individual's chronological age and the extent to which age affects the ability to adapt to new work situations and to do work in competition with others. The research that went into designing the regulations recognized that as a person grows older, their ability to adjust to a work setting becomes more difficult.

Research and professional experience in the field of rehabilitation has borne out the assumption that as people age, vocational adjustment to new work becomes more difficult. Sections 404.1563 and 416.963 of the regulations governing disability under the Social Security program separates age into these categories:

(a) **Younger Person** – if an individual is under age 50, the regulations provide that generally an individual's age will not seriously affect the ability to adapt to new work situations.

(b) **Person Approaching Advanced Age** – if an individual is closely approaching advanced age (50 -- 54), along with a severe impairment and limited work experience, age will be considered as possibly seriously affecting an individual's ability to adapt to a significant number of jobs.

(c) **Persons of Advanced Age** – advanced age (55-59) is considered to be the point at which age significantly affects a person's ability to engage in substantial gainful activity. If an individual is severely impaired, he/she may be found disabled unless the individual has skills that can be used in (transferred to) less demanding jobs.

(d) **Persons Close to Retirement** – if an individual is close to retirement age (60-64) and has a severe impairment, he/she will be considered unable to adjust to sedentary or light work unless the individual has skills that are highly marketable.

The criteria used by the Social Security Administration to determine the effects of age upon a person's ability to work does not mean a person with a severe impairment at any age cannot work. But the criteria does set forth some of the conditions vocational experts must consider in making an assessment of a claimant's ability to work. Basically, the regulations say that a younger person, under 50 years of age, should have no significant difficulty in adjusting to new work. With clients between 50 and 54, age may be a factor and seriously affect their ability to adjust to a "significant number" of alternative jobs. For claimants over 55 "age significantly affects a person's ability to work" unless they have work skills which can be transferred to other occupations. At ages 55 to 59 vocational experts need not only to consider vocational adjustment but also the kinds of work skills their client can carry over to new work. For persons age 60 and above, transferable work skills should be "highly marketable".

Factor # 2: Formal Education and Vocational Training:

In making a determination about a person's employability, age is only one of the vocational factors vocational experts need to consider. Generally, age is used only in regard to the ability of a person with impairments to make a vocational adjustment to alternative work. Age should not affect a person's ability to perform their past work unless other factors exist, such as the intrusion of a disability, reducing a person's RFC, a lengthy time period between the present and when the work was performed, or changes that may have occurred in the way the work is normally performed in the national economy. Occupational changes would become a consideration if, for instance, a person had been a retail clerk in an electronics store in the 1970's. The product knowledge learned in the remote past would be of little benefit to them in the same retail setting today.

A second factor in the determination of a vocational profile is the person's education and/or vocational training. Education primarily means formal schooling or other training which contributes to a person's intellectual ability to meet the requirements of a job or an occupation. The kinds of skill a person likely learned in a formal school setting include reasoning, communication skills, and arithmetical ability. However, a lack of formal schooling does not necessarily mean that a claimant is uneducated or lacks the abilities in reasoning, communication, and arithmetic. Duties and responsibilities from work done in the past may demonstrate intellectual abilities, although a claimant may have very little formal education.

How do vocational experts determine the reasoning, mathematics, and language requirements of a particular job? The *Dictionary of Occupational Titles*, pp. 1009 – 1012 provides what is known as the **General Education Scale (GED)** which lists the general intellectual abilities required of a worker for a satisfactory performance of a particular job. The categories provided are Reasoning Development, Mathematical Development, and Language Development. The intellectual requirements are described on a scale of one (1) to six (6), with one being the lowest level and six being the highest level. (The "Scale of General Educational Development" can be found in Appendix 7:3 of the *Dictionary of Occupational Titles*). Below each of the job descriptions listed in the DOT are references to each of the three categories. For instance, a Dining Room Attendant or Bus Person (311.667-018) needs to have a commonsense understanding to carry out detailed but uninvolved written or oral instructions (R2), add and subtract two digit numbers, as well as perform simple multiplication and division calculations (M1), and be able to read and speak simple sentences (L1).

The usefulness of a client's educational background may depend on (1) how much time has elapsed between the completion of formal education and the onset of a physical or mental impairment, and (2) what the person has done with their education at work or in life. Formal education that the person completed many years before, or long, unused skills and knowledge that were part of a person's formal education may no longer prove meaningful or useful in terms of their ability to work.

The Social Security Administration has listed educational categories in their regulations governing their disability programs. These categories reveal the functioning of persons at various educational levels and the kinds of work – unskilled, semi-skilled, and skilled – the person is likely to be able to enter given that level of intellectual functioning. The federal guidelines make these categories binding on vocational expert in disability hearings. In other words, a vocational expert (VE) in a disability hearing must consider the educational categories, listed below, in their evaluation of jobs and in a determination of jobs that claimant can do. The following descriptions of the categories as applied in the federal regulations are taken from the *Vocational Expert Handbook*, February, 2003.

Educational Categories:

1. **Illiterate or Unable to Communicate in English**: A person is illiterate if he or she cannot read or write a simple message

such as instructions or inventory lists, even though that person can sign his or her name. Generally, an illiterate individual has little or no formal schooling. A person who does not speak and understand English may find it difficult to perform a job, regardless of the amount of education the individual may have in another language. Therefore, the counselor should consider a person's ability to communicate in English when evaluating what work, if any, he or she can perform. Generally, the identity of another language which the person speaks fluently is immaterial.

2. **Marginal:** This category refers to formal schooling at the 6th grade level or below and the acquisition of reasoning, arithmetic, and language skills which permit performance of simple, unskilled work.

3. **Limited:** This term denotes formal schooling at the 7th grade through 11th grade level and reasoning, arithmetic, and language skills which do not permit performance of most of the more complex job duties needed in semi-skilled or skilled jobs.

4. **High School Education or More:** Generally speaking, this category is used for individuals who have completed the 12th

grade or have earned a high school equivalency diploma. Persons in this category have acquired the reasoning, language, and arithmetic skills which permit performance of semi-skilled and skilled work.

5. **High School Graduate or More - Provides for Direct Entry into Skilled Work:** This category applies when a short period of time has elapsed since the completion of formal education, which enables the individual with a minimal degree of job orientation, to begin performing the skilled job duties of certain identifiable occupations with their residual functional capacity (RFC)

Factor # 3: Work Experience

When representatives from the United States Employment Services (USES) performed their job analysis of each of the 12,791 jobs contained in the *Dictionary of Occupational Titles* (DOT), they looked at each job from the standpoint of the physical effort it took to perform the job and the skill required to learn the position and perform the work adequately or satisfactorily. Each of the jobs listed in the DOT has beneath the job description a symbol that designates the time required to learn the job, SVP, standing for Significant Vocational Preparation, and the amount of exertion required. For instance, a Collating-Machine Operator sets up and operates a machine that performs certain functions, such as assembling and perforating, stapling, gluing, folding or cutting sheets of paper. This position is listed at 653.382-104 on page 601 of the DOT. Beneath the job description is listed as Strength (L) and an SVP (4). This means that the exertion level for this job is light, requiring the worker to walk and stand at least six hours in an 8-hour day and lift up to 20 pounds occasionally and 10 pounds frequently. To learn the job duties of a Collating-Machine Operator at an SVP 4 level requires four to six months (see time levels listed below).

Vocational Experts classify past work of claimants and describe jobs that they believe claimants can perform given certain hypothetical situations in the same way. They examine the exertion level and the SVP level provided under the job description in the DOT for each job named in the hearing. (A discussion of the physical demands for work and the SVP required for each job can be found on pages 1009 to 1013 of the *Dictionary of Occupational Titles*).

Levels of Exertion

The level of exertion required for each job in the *Dictionary of Occupational Titles* is rated in one of the following five (5) categories.

Sedentary: Sedentary work involves lifting no more than 10 pounds at a time and occasionally lifting or carrying articles like docket files, ledgers, and small tools. Although sedentary jobs involve sitting, they also require a certain amount walking and standing to carry out job duties. Jobs are sedentary if they require occasional walking and/or occasional walking and standing, provided other sedentary criteria are met. Because sedentary occupations may require occasional standing and walking, the actual periods of standing or walking should generally total no more than 2 hours of an 8-hour workday. Sedentary work entails no significant stooping, but most unskilled sedentary jobs require repetitive hands and/or finger movements.

Light: Light work involves lifting no more than 20 pounds at a time with frequent lifting and carrying of objects weighing up to 10 pounds. Since frequent lifting or carrying requires a claimant to be on his or her feet up to 2/3 of a workday, the full range of light work requires standing or walking for a total of approximately 6 hours in an 8-hour workday. Sitting may occur intermittently during the remaining time. Even though the weight the claimant lifts in a particular light job may be minimal, the regulations classify a job as "light" when it requires a significant amount of walking or standing. Some light jobs, like sewing machine operator, though performed while sitting, involve pushing or pulling of hand or foot controls. However, light jobs generally do not involve the use of the fingers for fine manipulation to the extent required in most sedentary jobs.

Medium: Medium work involves lifting no more than 50 pounds at a time with frequent lifting and carrying of objects up to 25 pounds. A full range of medium work requires standing and walking for a total of approximately 6 hours in an 8-hour workday. Medium work generally requires only use of the hands and arms to grasp, hold, or turn objects. Medium jobs require considerable lifting and frequent bending or stooping.

Heavy: Heavy work involves lifting no more than 100 pounds at a time with frequent lifting or carrying of objects weighing up to 50 pounds.

Very Heavy: Very heavy work involves frequently lifting objects weighing 150 pounds or more.

Significant Vocational Preparation (SVP)

As stated above, each of the jobs listed in the DOT also has a SVP designation that classifies each job in the time it takes to learn the job tasks and perform the position adequately or satisfactorily. The time spans are divided into nine categories. These categories are:

Level Time

1.   Short Duration Only

2.   Anything beyond Short Demonstration up to and including a month

3.   Over 1 month up to and including 3 months

4.   Over 3 months up to and including 6 months.

5.   Over six months up to and including 1 year

6.   Over 1 year up and including 2 years

7.   Over 2 years up to and including 4 years

8.   Over 4 years up and to including 10 years

9.   Over 10 years

Identification of Work Skills:

As stated above, the amount of time it takes to learn a job is called **Specific Vocational Preparation (SVP).** (The *Dictionary of Occupational Titles* lists these (9) categories in Appendix C on p. 1009 of the *Dictionary of Occupational Titles* (DOT). The level of each job can be found below the job description in the DOT following the General Educational Development designations). The *Dictionary of Occupational Titles* provides an SVP for each of the 12, 741 jobs listed. For instance, the job listing for Maintenance Supervisor is on page 282 of the DOT. The SVP for the Maintenance Supervisor is a level 6. In an analysis of this position in 1977 (DUI), the job analyst for the Department of Labour found that for a worker to learn the job of Maintenance Supervisor and reach an adequate or satisfactory level of performance takes one to two years. This work, therefore, is considered a skilled occupation.

The federal regulations governing the administration of the disability program for Social Security defines a skill as "knowledge of a work activity which requires (1) the exercise of significant judgment that goes beyond the carrying out of simple job duties and (2) is acquired through performance of an occupation which is above the unskilled level. A skill is made up of the practical and familiar knowledge of the principles and processes of an art, science, or trade, combined with the ability to apply them in practice in a proper and approved manner. This includes activities like making precise measurements, reading blueprints, and setting up and operating complex machinery.

Skills are divided into three (3) categories. These are:

1. **Unskilled Work**. Unskilled occupations are the least complex types of work. Unskilled work needs little of no judgment to do simple duties that can be learned in less than 30 days, requires little specific vocational preparation, and little or no judgment. The job of a construction laborer may be an example of unskilled work. The significant vocational preparation (SVP) at levels 1 & 2 are considered unskilled occupations.

2. **Semi-Skilled Work**. Semi-skilled occupations are more complex than unskilled work and distinctly simpler than the more highly skilled types of jobs. Semi-skilled work needs some skills but does not require doing the more complex job duties. Jobs in the semi-skilled range require learning (schooling and/ or on-the-job training) from one month to six months in duration. The significant vocational preparation (SVP) at levels 3 & 4 are considered semi-skilled occupations.

3. **Skilled Work**. Skilled occupations are more complex and varied than unskilled and semi-skilled occupations. They require more training time and often a higher educational attainment. Abstract thinking in specialized fields may be required, as for chemists and architects. Special artistic talents and mastery of a musical instrument may be involved, as for school band instructors and understanding of charts and technical manuals may be needed by an automobile mechanic. The president or chief executive office of a business organization may need exceptional ability to deal with people, organize various data, and make difficult decisions in several areas of knowledge. The significant vocational preparation (SVP) at levels 5 through 9 are considered skilled occupations.

References

1 "Annual Statistical Report on the Social Security Disability

Insurance Program, Office of Retirement and Disability Policy,

Social Security Administration, 2008, September 23, 2009, Pg. 1-

11.

2 Blackwell, Terry L., Field, Timothy, and Field, Janet (1992). *The*

Vocational Expert Under Social Security, Athens, Georgia: Elliott &

Fitzpatrick.

3 Department of Labor, *Employment and Training Administration*

(1991) *Revised Handbook for Analyzing Jobs:. Reprinted and*

distributed by Jist Works, Inc. Indianapolis, IN.

4 Department of Labor, *Employment and Training Administration*

(*1992). Selected Characteristics of Occupations* defined in the

Dictionary of Occupational Titles

5 Ellwood, P.M., Jr. (1968). "Can We Afford So Many Rehabilitation

Professions." *Journal of Rehabilitation*, 34(3), pp. 21-22.

6 Fields, Timothy F., and Sink, Jack M. (January 1981). The

Vocational Expert. VBS, Inc.,

7 A History of the Social Security Disability Programs: (1986). Disability History Report (1986) Social Security Administration, pg. 1-10.

8. History of the Social Security During the Johnson Administration, 1963-1968: Vocational Expert Program", Social Security Administration, pg. 1-7.

9 Hubley, Nathaniel O. (2008). "The Untouchables: Why a Vocational Expert's Testimony in Social Security Disability Hearings Cannot be Touched." Valparaiso University Law Review, Number 1, Volume 43, 353-406, Fall.

10 Kearsey, John R., (2006) Social Security and the "D" in OASDI: The History of a Federal Program Insuring Earners Against Disability,"

11 SkillTRAN Data Resources (2001-2005). A History of the Social Security Disability Programs, Social Security Administration.

12 United States Department of Labor, Employment, and Training Administration, 4th Ed. (1991). *Dictionary of Occupational Titles*

13 Vercillo, Amy, (2012) *Social Security Vocational Expert Most
Common Hypotheticals*" a presentation at the International
Association of Rehabilitation Professionals Conference in Puerto
Rico.

14 Vocational Expert Handbook, 2nd Ed. (2003). Office of the Chief
Judge, Philadelphia Region, Social Security Administration.

15 Vocational Expert Handbook, November (2010) Office of
Disability Adjudication and Review, Office of the Chief
Administrative Law Judge.

Other Books by the Authors

Asheley D. Wells, MS, CRC
& Gerald K. Wells, Ph.D., CRC

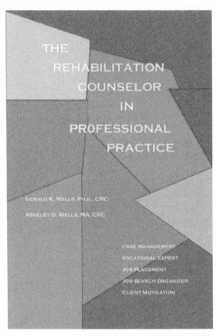

**The Rehabilitation
Counselor
in Professional Practice**
By Gerald K. Wells, Ph.D.,
CRC
& Asheley D. Wells, MS,
CRC

The Rehabilitation Counselor in Professional Practice is about the everyday ins and outs in vocational counselling with our clients: making job decisions, teaching job-seeking skills, and choosing strategies for helping persons with disabilities locate the best jobs available, given their functional limitations. In this text practicing rehabilitation counsellors share what they have learned from their education and experience about vocational counselling and job placement to achieve employment goals for their clients.

http://www.aspenprofessionalservices.com/

Job Search Organizer
By Gerald K. Wells, Ph.D., CRC
& Asheley D. Wells, MS, CRC

What makes the 'The Job Search Organizer" original and different from any other job-search material is that it is uniquely shaped to the needs of the field of rehabilitation. Before and during the job search, the Organizer becomes a management strategy and discussion document to help counsellors identify important information, recognize and reinforce motivators and success behaviors, surface traits and client achievements important to employers, teach job-seeking skills, and manage the overall job-search process. The Job Search Organizer:

- Reinforces the role of the counselor as manager.

- Focuses a counselor's time upon those who want to work and who are most likely to benefit most from rehabilitation services.

- Requires that clients become involved in their own job search.

- Focuses the content of the counselling sessions to help counsellors manage their time.

- Provides a networking plan for clients that surfaces job contacts and job leads.

Most important, "The Job-Search Organizer" addresses the need for uniformity in job placement. Too often in the field of rehabilitation we throw away the accumulated experience from our past and begin the next day with a clean slate. While there are unique features to every job search, there is much common ground and known knowledge in how to look for and secure jobs for our clients. No rehabilitation counselor should have to begin a job search without the benefit of experience from those who have gone before. And no new rehabilitation counselor should have to become involved in a job search without professional guidance.

http://www.rehabilitationcounselinngbooks.com

Made in United States
Orlando, FL
02 October 2024

52216292R10093